OKLAHOMA

OKLAHOMA BY ROAD

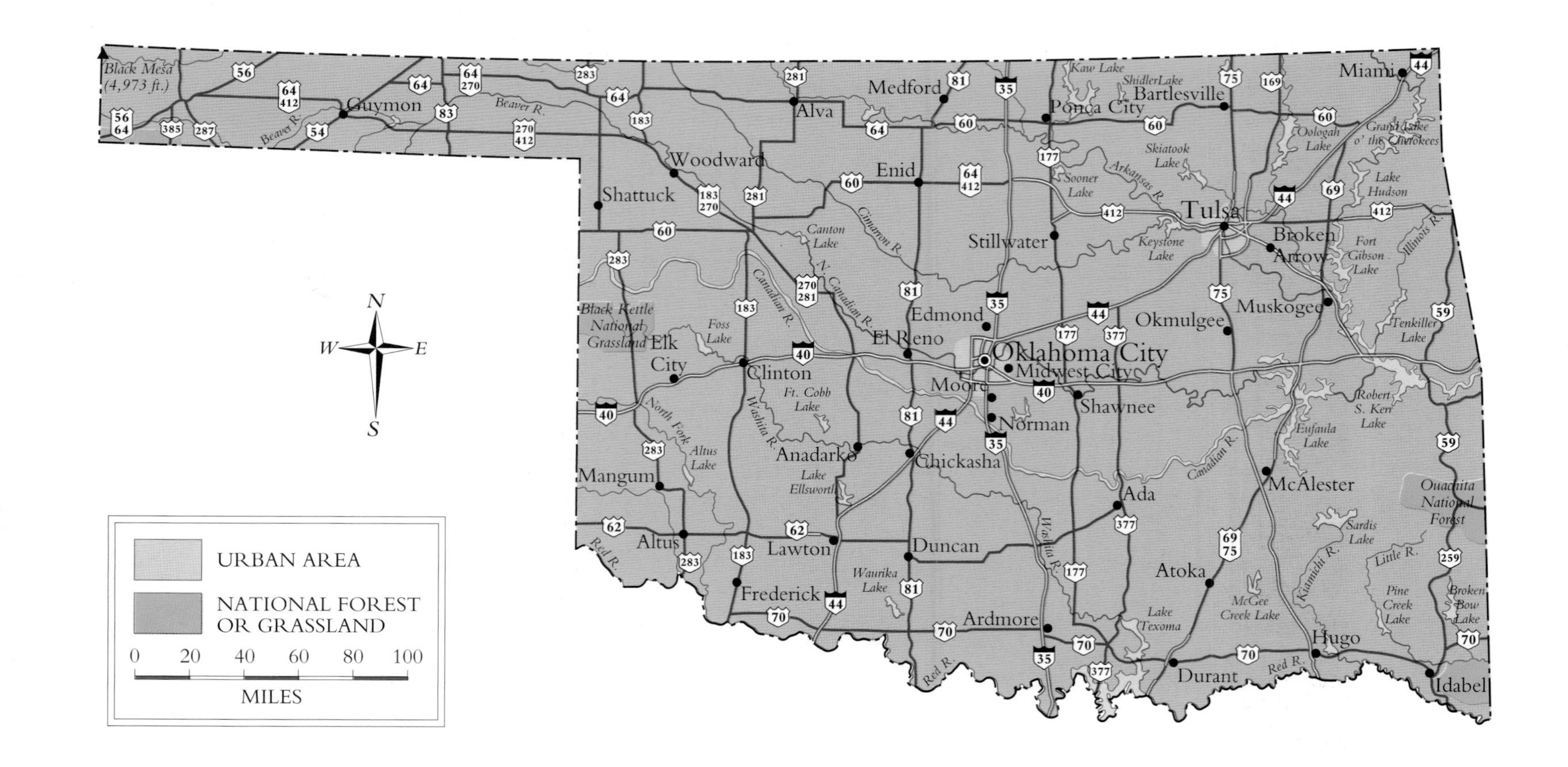

CELEBRATE THE STATES

OKLAHOMA

Guy Baldwin

Benchmark Books

MARSHALL CAVENDISH
NEW YORK

Benchmark Books
Marshall Cavendish Corporation
99 White Plains Road
Tarrytown, New York 10591-9001

Library of Congress Cataloging-in-Publication Data

Baldwin, Guy.
Oklahoma / Guy Baldwin.
p. cm. — (Celebrate the states)
Includes bibliographical references and index.
ISBN 0-7614-1067-8
1. Oklahoma—Juvenile literature. [1. Oklahoma.} I. Title. II. Series.
F694.3 .B36 2001 976.6—dc21 00-036099

Maps and graphics supplied by Oxford Cartographers, Oxford, England

Photo Research by Candlepants Incorporated

Cover Photo: Jim Argo

The photographs in this book are used by permission and through the courtesy of; *Jim Argo*: 6-7, 16, 22, 24, 25, 58, 74, 84-85, 101, 104, 106, 107, 110, 112, 126 (top), 135, back cover. *Corbis* : Jim Sugar, 10-11; William A. Bake, 13; David Muench, 14; Perry Conway, 20 (bottom); Danny Lehman, 48-49; Peter Turnley, 53, 66-67, 90; Eric & David Hosking, 56; Annie Griffiths Belt, 57; Arthur Rothstein, 63; Jack Fields, 64; David Bartruff, 71, 115; Ted Spiegel, 80; Joseph Sohm; Chromosohm Inc., 83; Bettmann, 92, 129 (right), 132 (left), 134 (top); Tom Bean, 98-99; Susan Middleton & David Litschwager, 123; AFP, 128; S.I.N., 129 (left); Lynn Goldsmith, 132(right); Hulton Deutsch Collection, 133; 96. *Photo Researchers*: Leonard Lee Rue, 20 (top), 122; Lawrence Migdale, 61, 72; Frank W. Mantlik, 119 (left); Gilbert Grant, 119(right). *Oklahoma Tourism* : Fred Marvel, 21, 69, 77, 79, 81, 114, 117, 126 (left). *Oklahoma City Museum, Oklahoma City, Oklahoma*: 26-27. *National Museum of American Art, Washington DC/Art Resource NY*: 30. *The Thomas Gilcrease Institute of American History and Art, Tulsa Oklahoma*: 31. *Oklahoma Historical Society*: 32, 38, 39, 43, 47. *Western History Collection, University of Oklahoma Libraries*: 36, 40, 44, 45. *Photograph copyright May 26,1989, The Oklahoma Publishing Company*: 87. *Woody Guthrie Archive/photo by Robin Carson*: 94. *Archive Photos*: Bernard Gotfryd, 130; Kostos Alexander/Fotos International, 134 (lower).

Printed in Italy

3 5 6 4 2

CONTENTS

OKLAHOMA IS . . .

Oklahoma is a place that people love to call home.

I've got the Oklahoma blues,
the blues that I can't lose.
Gonna settle down in a one-horse town
and throw away my shoes!
Where the sun comes up in the wintertime
and shines across the snow—
It's the best by test in the wooly West
and it's where I've got to go.
—Jimmy Weekly and His Rough Riders, "The Oklahoma Blues"

"We were there. High up the trees flurried with birdsong, and one clear note sang above the rest, a lucid, soaring strand of sound; . . . I breathed deeply the blossoms and sunlight and there was a sigh in it. I thought, Here is the place to stay, grow up with the state, take root." —novelist Ralph Ellison

Oklahoma is expansive.

"Oklahoma is tallgrass prairie and everlasting mountains. It is secret patches of ancient earth tromped smooth and hard by generations of dancing feet. It is the cycle of song and heroic deed. It is calloused hands. It is the aroma of rich crude oil fused with the scent of sweat and sacred smoke." —writer Michael Wallis

"I'm from Oklahoma—I need space!" —model Amber Valletta

Oklahoma has a rich, contradictory history.

"It is difficult to set down the solemn facts about Oklahoma without their reading like something copied out of an insane encyclopedia." —writer George Milburn

Its people deal stoutheartedly with hard conditions.

"No question about it. We take it on the chin, but we don't give in."
—television meteorologist Gary England

Oklahoma is a young state—the forty-sixth to join the nation. But it has pressed a lot into its short history. A combination of unusual land, unusual people, and unusual circumstances makes it one of the oddest and most interesting of the American states. It's a place that rewards those who stop to learn about its history, its people, and its ways of life. Let's explore Oklahoma.

1 HIGH PLAINS AND ROCKY HOLLOWS

On a map, Oklahoma resembles a jagged butcher's cleaver slicing into Texas. The strip in the northwest is the handle, and the wiggly line to the south—the Red River—is the knife edge. The state also shares borders with New Mexico to the west, Kansas and Colorado to the north, and Missouri and Arkansas to the east.

ONE STATE, MANY REGIONS

Oklahoma's borders enclose a rich mishmash of landscapes. Forested foothills and low mountains shape the northeast, where the Ozarks, with their tall pines and twisty valleys, reach into the state. The Arbuckle and Wichita ranges in the south are rougher and more rugged. Volcanic pressure pushing up from inside the earth caused these granite peaks to rise. We only see the tips of them today. Geologist Charles Gould wrote that the Wichitas are "nothing but the tops of buried mountain ranges projecting above and surrounded by a sea of plain." The Ouachita range in the southeast is a mass of narrow slabs of yellow sandstone set on edge. These peaks are cloaked by forests of loblolly pine and cedar and dotted with spring-fed lakes.

The Cross Timbers, a belt of hilly woodland, separates the rolling east from the flatter plains of the west. Here the land rises and twists like a rumpled bedspread. Taller varieties of oak, along with

The Ouachitas are among the wildest and most remote mountains in Oklahoma. Folding, faults, and erosion all played a part in producing the distinctive look of this part of the state.

hickories and pecans, poke above a cover of short, scrubby black-jack oaks.

West of the Cross Timbers, Oklahoma eases into prairieland. The plains seem flat at first glance, but a closer look reveals sudden woodlands, hidden gullies, and abrupt swells of exposed rock. Of the Oklahoma plains, journalist Phil Brown writes, "We can see from horizon to horizon with the exception of the forests of blackjack trees growing so closely together that it looks as if it would be

Tallgrass prairie once covered 400,000 square miles in the United States. Less than 1 percent remains. The Tallgrass Prairie Preserve in northeastern Oklahoma is one of the largest and best-preserved examples that endures. It is home to more than seven hundred plant species and a growing herd of bison.

difficult to walk through them." As long as the rain falls, wheat and cotton thrive here on the rich soil.

These fertile plains blend into the higher, harsher plains of the northwest and the Panhandle—the narrow strip of land that juts west from the rest of the state. This is an area as complicated as the beat-up surface of an old table. Gray gypsum and red sandstone peek through the thin soil like old layers of paint, and rivers cut wavy scratches across the land. Cottonwood, willow, and tamarisk trees huddle in the river lowlands. Higher up, prairie grasses cover much of the plains. This landscape "has a thorny personality," says Oklahoma geologist Gary Thompson. Its plants and animals are "designed to puncture, penetrate, and poison"—from diamond-back rattlesnakes and horned toads to prickly pear cactus, burrs, and spiky thickets of wild plums.

WATERWAYS

Oklahoma has hundreds of rivers and creeks, but two really stand out: the Red River, which meanders along its southern border, and the Arkansas River in the northeast, which is important for shipping. Since dams, dredging, and channel widening were completed in 1970, the Arkansas River Navigation System has opened shipping traffic from the Mississippi River as far west as Tulsa. Ships can sail to Tulsa from any ocean in the world, making it one of America's most important inland ports.

While Oklahoma's eastern rivers tend to flow deeply through well-defined channels, its western rivers and streams behave quite differently. They flow more irregularly and carry far more sand,

Coal barges negotiate the Arkansas River east of Tulsa. Since the Arkansas River Navigation System opened in 1970, the river has become a major transportation artery linking Oklahoma to the Mississippi River and, by connection, to the world.

clay, and gravel. As the water cuts a channel, these materials fill it in again. The result is wide, shallow, muddy rivers such as the Cimarron, Canadian, and Washita which can spill from one channel to another when there is a lot of water and dry up completely when there isn't.

Oklahoma has more than one hundred natural lakes, but humans have made even more. Dams and diversions have created

WHERE'S THE BORDER?

The wriggling, muddy, disorderly Red River forms the southern border of Oklahoma. Where the land is flat, the river often changes course, jumping its bank to follow new channels. Every time this happens, part of Texas becomes part of Oklahoma, or the other way around.

This stretch of river has been baffling bordermakers for centuries. Spain and the United States argued about it when the United States acquired the area north of the river in 1803. During the 1920s, Texas Rangers and the Oklahoma National Guard nearly clashed over the issue. Tax collectors, law enforcement officials, and wildlife managers in both states scratched their heads every time the river moved, wondering who was now responsible for the nearby land.

The two states studied the problem for years. In 1999, they finally agreed that the boundary should be on the south bank of the river along the "vegetation line," where trees and bushes have grown along the river's usual path. "It solves problems that have plagued citizens of the Red River valley for almost 200 years," says Bill Abney, a Texan who helped negotiate the solution.

The Red River isn't changing its wandering ways. But now when it shifts course the two states will know what to do about it—though they may have to wait for a few years to see where the new vegetation line grows.

two hundred artificial lakes in the state—partly for recreation, but also to control flooding and to supply hydroelectric power. One of the largest is Lake Tenkiller, whose clear waters attract boaters and anglers—and scuba divers, who enjoy an underwater "playground" built just for them.

LAND AND WATER

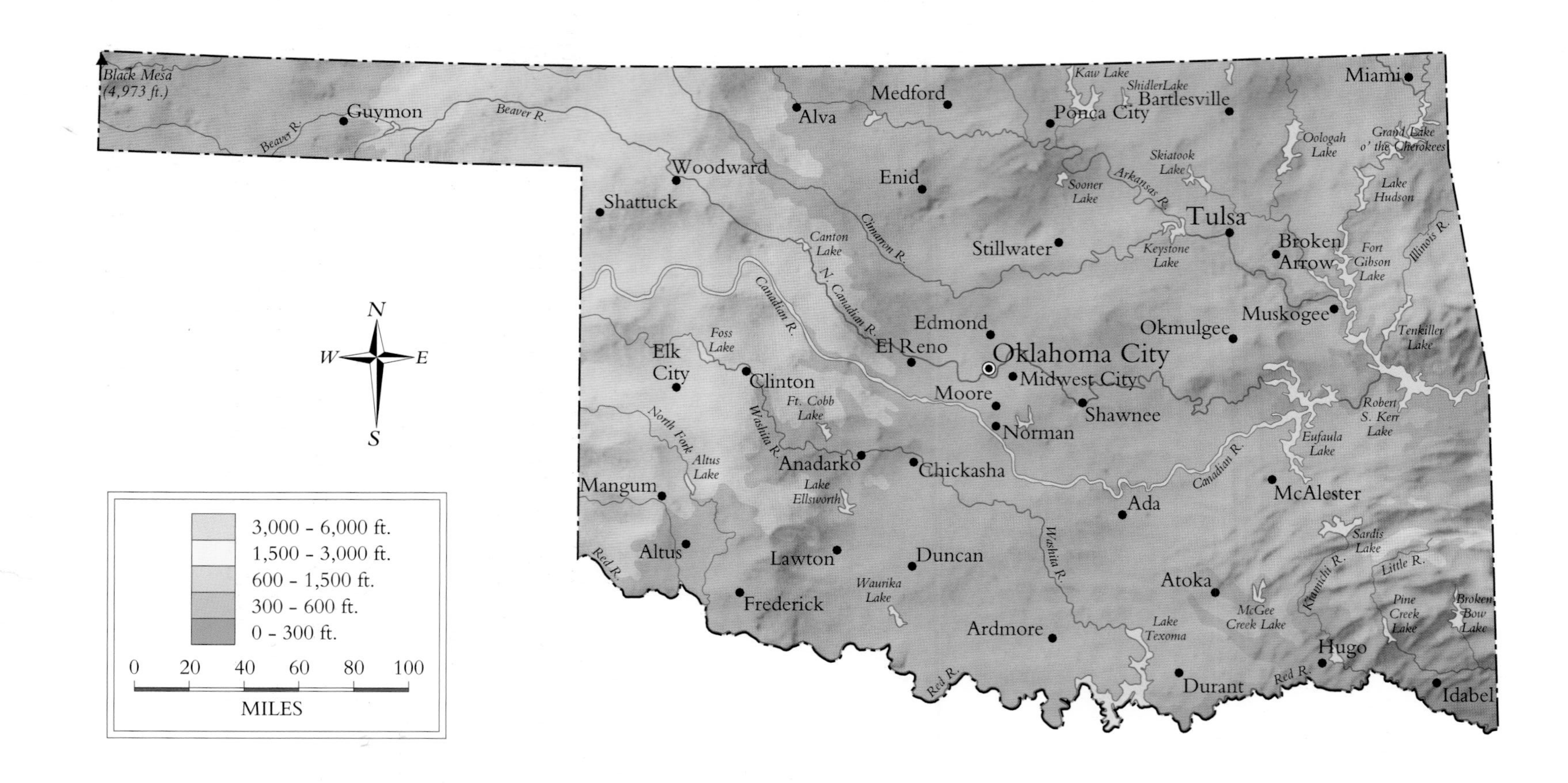

A LIVELY LANDSCAPE

Oklahoma's varied landscape provides homes for a complex mix of plants and animals. Deer, moose, elk, and antelope roam prairie lands; bears and coyotes can also be found. The state's smaller animals include armadillos, opossums, and rabbits.

Lakes and streams support catfish, bass, perch, sunfish, and trout. A wide range of birds call Oklahoma home. These include the roadrunner and the scissor-tailed flycatcher, Oklahoma's state bird.

Near the northwestern town of Freedom, plumes of what look like dark, sooty smoke rise at sunset on the horizon. At daybreak, the same occurs in reverse, as if the earth were sucking the smoke back in. But it's not smoke. It's bats, about a million of them. They belong to one of the largest bat colonies in the United States. They sleep in caves by day and rise at night to hunt, eating ten tons of insects every night. Bat viewing events are held at the caves during the summer.

Before the plow, much of Oklahoma was covered with native prairie grasses, the tallest growing where the most rain fell. But farmers plowed under all but a few bits of it. The Tallgrass Prairie Preserve north of Pawhuska is one of the last large patches of this magnificent windswept grassland. Vast herds of bison lived on this land before they were hunted nearly to extinction in the nineteenth century. A new bison herd, established in the early 1990s, is helping to restore the original ecology of this area.

Even driving by at high speed, visitors to Oklahoma will notice what look like big, messy birds' nests in the branches of many trees. A closer look reveals the state flower: mistletoe. The state is

The pronghorn antelope is the fastest of North America's mammals. It can hit speeds of more than sixty miles an hour.

Oklahoma is home to the opossum, North America's only member of the marsupial family (marsupials are animals, such as kangaroos, with pouches in which they raise their newborn young). They prefer wooded habitat close to water—so most of the state's "possums" are found in the east.

UNDERDOGS OF THE PLAINS

Not long ago, Oklahoma's prairielands featured vast prairie dog towns—fields speckled with openings to an underground network of tunnels and dens, created and tended by cute but ferocious little rodents. "They can bite through welder's gloves," says wildlife expert Rebecca Fischer. "Their giant incisors [teeth] are like little chisels."

Ranchers often despise prairie dogs for eating the grass, chewing fenceposts, and digging holes that have left many a horse with a broken leg. Trapping, shooting, poisoning, development, and disease have wiped out 99 percent of the creatures nationwide.

Today, prairie dogs are on the rebound in Oklahoma. Scientists have discovered that they support plants and other animals in the prairie ecosystem. Because of their digging, weedy plants take over from grass. These plants are sought out by cattle, bison, antelope, and elk for their high nutrition.

Naturalists are helping to reestablish prairie dog towns in places like the Martin Nature Center in Oklahoma City, but other creatures like badgers don't make it easy. Badgers are "earth-moving machines with teeth," says naturalist Neil Garrison, and "prairie dogs are like a one-pound sausage." A prairie dog town defends itself by constant vigilance. It's full of lookouts—individual animals peering about and sniffing the air for signs of danger. When one spies trouble it spreads the alarm, and all duck for cover into their maze of holes and tunnels.

a major supplier of the mistletoe sprigs that Christmas kissers stand under.

WILD WEATHER

Oklahoma is well known for its varied and violent weather. Every spring tornadoes sweep the state, causing people to dive for the safety of their basements. Damage to buildings is often enormous. "I've always wanted skylights," joked Marian Keef after a twister

Bison once ranged across all of Oklahoma. They are now making a comeback in places like the Wichita Mountains Wildlife Refuge near Lawton.

ripped the roof off her bedroom. Her husband, Ron, put the damage in perspective: "We've got nothing to gripe about. We're alive, and we're not hurt."

They were lucky. Some of the worst tornadoes in memory hit central Oklahoma in the spring of 1999, including one near Mulhall that appeared to be a mile wide. In a matter of minutes a thousand houses near Oklahoma City were flattened. More than forty people died.

From atop a fire station, firefighter Jerry Doshier watched the storm rip the roof off his house; then he saw his wife, Karen, emerge from the wreckage. "Something like this shows you, all of this stuff, all of this rubble, it's just things, it's just stuff. It doesn't mean anything," he said. "It's only people that mean anything. . . . See, that's my truck over there, that Dodge. Do you want it? Here's the key. It doesn't mean anything. People have to know that."

Because of its severe weather, Oklahoma is home to the National Severe Storms Laboratory and the Storm Prediction Center, which have helped turn the art of storm forecasting into a science. Gary England, a television meteorologist, remembers when the only clue that a tornado was approaching was when "it blew down your friend's house up the road." Now, sophisticated equipment like Doppler radar helps England get the word out about dangerous weather in time to save lives.

THIS DUSTY OLD DUST

Another weather hazard is drought. During the summer of 1998, many farmers lost their crops because of low rainfall. Rancher

Truman Zybach had to sell his cattle because he couldn't feed them. "We're plum out of green grass," he lamented. All across Oklahoma the fields baked dry. Farmers squinted at fields of bare, parched soil. "We probably haven't seen in most of our lifetimes a drought this severe," reflected Pat McDowell of the Oklahoma Agriculture Department.

Real old-timers, however, have hardly forgotten the terrible droughts of the 1930s—the legendary Dust Bowl years. By plowing

Doppler radar systems, such as this one in Norman, can measure the speed and direction of storms and their intensity. With Doppler radar, weather forecasters are better able to predict severe weather and save lives.

During droughts, farmers and their animals suffer alike. When dry spells kill vegetation and parch the soil, the wind can whip up a desertlike landscape, as on this hog farm near Guymon.

away the hardy, drought-resistant prairie grasses and replacing them with wheat and cotton, farmers exposed the soil to the wind and water erosion. During a series of dry years, much of western Oklahoma's topsoil blew away. It was one of the worst environmental disasters in American history.

Droughts are simply a natural condition in the state. "Oklahoma is on the edge of an arid zone," says Pat McDowell. Dry years still mean the loss of the fertile topsoil, but farmers have learned to lessen this by plowing along the contours of the land and by rotating what they plant so that a single crop doesn't wear out the soil. Like all Oklahomans, they've come to appreciate their land's ornery behavior. More than ever, they strive to adapt to the land—rather than the other way around.

2 SOONER AND LATER

Fall in Oklahoma, *by Oscar Jacobson*

Jacobson
1954

"Although it was one of the last of the states to enter the Union, Oklahoma has in one sense the most unusual history of them all," remarks historian Lawrence Goodwyn. The flags of Spain, France, Mexico, the Republic of Texas, and the Confederate States of America have flown there. Dozens of Indian tribes have followed as many different trails to the state. Oklahoma combines get-rich-quick stories of land rushes and oil booms with the hardscrabble lives of sharecroppers and the Dust Bowl tragedy. Between these extremes are countless stories of ordinary people building lives and communities.

EARLY OKLAHOMA

Recorded history covers only a tiny part of human experience in Oklahoma. People began living there at least 11,000 years ago. They were nomadic people who moved from place to place following game. About 2,500 years ago they began settling down and growing crops. Scientists have found ruined villages built of sandstone slabs, scattered with animal bones and stone tools and surrounded by fields where corn, beans, and squash had once grown. Spiro Mounds, in eastern Oklahoma, seems to have been an important political and religious center between eight hundred and one thousand years ago. It belonged to a system of communities that traded with others as far away as the Great Lakes and the Pacific Ocean. Spiro was abandoned before 1450 for reasons that are not clear—perhaps the climate grew drier and made it difficult to survive there.

The first written record of Oklahoma dates to 1541, when the Spanish explorer Francisco Vásquez de Coronado led an army across the future state's Panhandle on a fruitless search for gold. The armored soldiers must have been a bizarre sight to the people they encountered—probably the Wichita farmers and hunters whose villages dotted the area. Most of Oklahoma's people then were members of the Caddo confederation and lived in what would become the southeast corner of the state. Osage and Quapaw Indians lived farther north, while Apache communities followed the bison herds in the west. Comanches and Kiowas also arrived in the years before the United States took control.

So did other newcomers: missionaries and explorers from Spanish Mexico, and later, French fur traders. What they brought changed the Indians' ways of life. The Europeans' horses and guns transformed how the Indians hunted, traveled, and made war. The newcomers also brought deadly diseases such as smallpox and tuberculosis that had been unknown in Oklahoma.

INDIAN TERRITORY

In the late eighteenth century, the American Revolution put a new power into the mix. The United States, spreading out from the Atlantic coast, looked west for opportunities to expand. It got its chance in 1803 when France sold it the Louisiana Territory—the vast western lands whose rivers drained into the Mississippi River.

Oklahoma was part of that territory. Almost immediately, the Americans made their presence felt. Zebulon Pike led an American expedition into the area in 1806. He was followed by trappers, traders, and adventurers keen to discover what Oklahoma had to offer. The U.S. Army arrived in the 1820s, building Forts Gibson and Towson to protect its claims from Mexico, which owned neighboring Texas. The army would build half a dozen more forts in Oklahoma during the next four decades.

But it would be awhile before white settlers followed. In the 1830s, the United States decided that the area would become a

Clermont, chief of the Osages, led his people against American settlers and other Indians pushing west into the future Oklahoma. He was forced to cede his tribe's land to the United States in 1825, giving the United States its first firm foothold in the area. Painting by George Catlin.

Fort Gibson, established in 1824, was then the westernmost outpost of the U.S. government. Painting by Vincent Colyer.

territory for Indians "for as long as the grass should grow and the waters flow." Tribes expelled from the eastern states would be forced to accept land in this Indian Territory. Until the promise was broken at the end of the century, Indian Territory was a place uniquely separate from the rest of the United States.

The relocation of these tribes to Indian Territory is one of the most distressing chapters of American history. Whole communities were forced to walk cross-country at gunpoint, abandoning their land and possessions and enduring enormous hardship along the way. One-third of the Cherokee Nation died on the "Trail of Tears," as they called the route from their eastern homes to Indian Territory. The Choctaw, Creek, Seminole, and Chickasaw tribes followed similar hard trails to an uncertain future.

John Burnett was an army private who accompanied the Cherokee on the Trail of Tears. "I witnessed the execution of the most brutal order in the history of American warfare," he later recalled. "Future generations will read and condemn the act, and I do hope posterity will remember that private soldiers like myself . . . had to execute the orders of our superiors. We had no choice in the matter."

Working with very little, though, these "Five Civilized Tribes" adapted remarkably well to their strange new home. The Cherokees and Choctaws became prosperous cotton growers. Creeks became hog and cattle farmers, as did the Chickasaws, who also herded goats and sheep. The tribes had flour mills, sawmills, and cotton gins, and traded with nearby settlers and even their old enemy, the U.S. government.

BLOODBATH AND AFTERMATH

Then came the Civil War. In 1861, many Southern states rebelled against the Union over the issue of slavery and formed the Confederate States of America. The bloody "war between the states" was also fought in the territories, and for four years Indian Territory was a battle zone. Several of the newly arrived tribes had long owned African slaves. Partly for this reason, many Indians decided to support the slaveholding Confederacy when the Civil War began. Both the Union and the Confederacy sought the Indians' support and coveted their food, their horses, and the lead they mined for bullets. Ten thousand people—a fifth of the population of Indian Territory—died in the war or of the disease and starvation that followed it.

Indian Territory never really recovered from the war. At its beginning, tribes such as the Cherokees were "the wealthiest people in the West," wrote observer J. H. Beadle. "In 1865 their country was almost a waste; the people in extreme poverty. But they came back from the war and sadly went to work again." To punish tribes for their support of the rebels, the United States took away much of their land and assigned it to tribes it was driving out of other parts of the country. Pawnees, Peorias, Ottawas, Wyandots, and Miamis took up residence as farmers. But Cheyennes, Kiowas, Comanches, and Arapahos who were used to ranging over large hunting grounds had more difficulty adjusting to life on small reservations. By the end of this second wave of relocations, more than twenty tribes had reservations in Indian Territory.

American citizens were still barred from settling in Indian Territory, but their presence grew greater with every passing year. Ranchers from Texas began driving cattle across the territory to the railheads in Kansas. Others arrived to mine coal to fuel the trains. The tribes allowed these intrusions in exchange for money. They also sold residency permits to miners so they could live

THE OLD CHISHOLM TRAIL

"The Old Chisholm Trail" was the "hit song" of the 1870s. It starts out with the age-old ballad singer's invitation to "listen to my tale" and proceeds through literally hundreds of two-line verses to tell the tale of every adventure and misadventure that befell cowboys and their cattle as they made their way north on the trail from Texas through Oklahoma on their way to the slaughterhouses and railroad depot in Abilene, Kansas.

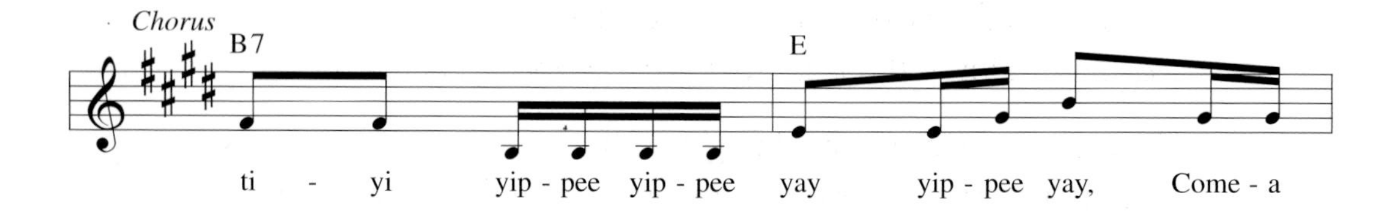

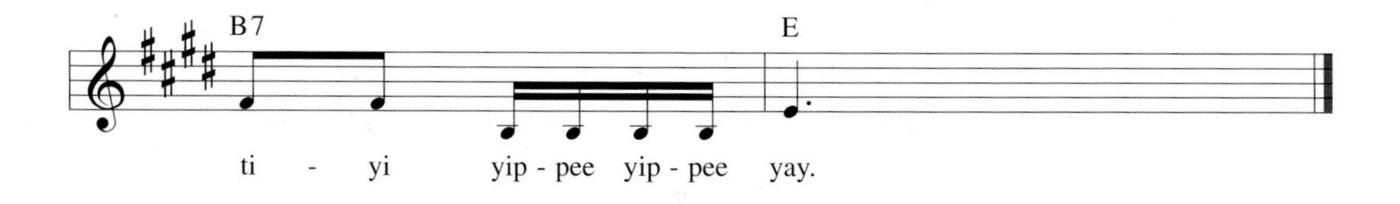

I started up the trail October twenty-third,
I started up the trail with the 2-U heard. *Chorus*

On a ten-dollar horse and a forty-dollar saddle,
I'm a-going to punch them Texas cattle. *Chorus*

I jumped in the saddle and grabbed a-holt the horn,
Best durn cowboy ever was born. *Chorus*

I'm up in the morning before delight,
And before I sleep the moon shines bright. *Chorus*

It's bacon and beans 'most every day,
I'd as soon be eating prairie hay. *Chorus*

Cloudy in the east and it looks like rain,
And my damned old slicker's in the wagon again. *Chorus*

Wing began to flow—rain began to fall,
It looked, by grab, like we was gonna lose 'em all. *Chorus*

I went to the boss to draw my roll,
He had me figured out nine dollars in the hole. *Chorus*

So me and the boss we had a little chat,
And I hit him in the face wuth my big slouch hat. *Chorus*

So the boss said to me, "I'm gonna fire you—
And not only you but the whole damn crew." *Chorus*

Well, I'm going back home to draw my money,
Going back home to see my honey. *Chorus*

Well, my feet are in the saddle and my saddle's in the sky,
And I'll quit punching cows in the Sweet Bye and Bye. *Chorus*

The opening of Indian Territory to outside settlement was accomplished as much by the railroads as by homesteaders. Railroads made or broke the futures of the towns they linked or bypassed. Here, the Atchison, Topeka, and Santa Fe Railroad builds into Tonkawa in 1899.

in the territory, but permit sales soon got out of control. Indian leaders could make a fast dollar by selling access to anyone who asked for it, and that's just what some of them did. As a result, Indian Territory became home to a growing number of "boomers" during the 1870s and 1880s.

Soon the railroads were laying tracks across Indian Territory. These powerful companies wanted a string of non-Indian towns along the rails to make their businesses more profitable. Boomers, too, clamored to be allowed to settle in Indian Territory. "Our people believe," declared Representative James Burnes to Congress, "that if it is lawful for a man with a vast herd of cattle to go into that territory, it is lawful for the settler to go there with his wife and little ones." Congress also listened to government officials in charge of Indian affairs who hoped that allowing open settlement would help destroy Indian traditions and force Indians to adapt to the American lifestyle. By the late 1880s, a movement was underway to take Indian Territory away from the Indians.

LAND RUSH

In 1887, the grass still grew and the water still flowed, but that year the U.S. government broke the "permanent" agreements it had made a half-century earlier. It decided to carve tribal lands in Indian Territory into 160-acre allotments and distribute them to individual Indian owners. The remaining land in Indian Territory would be opened to outside settlers.

There was no stopping this plan once it started. Some of the "surplus" land was awarded to homesteaders by lottery. The rest was offered to whoever claimed it first in a series of famous land rushes. The first of these began on April 22, 1889. Guns fired at noon, and fifty thousand settlers raced from the border to stake their claims. Some arrived at likely spots to find camps that were obviously more than a few hours old—they'd been beaten by settlers who'd jumped the gun. A few of these "sooners" were ejected, but plenty were not. Despised at first for their dishonesty, the sooners were later celebrated in Oklahoma folklore for their frontier cunning.

By the end of the day, all the land at the center of present-day Oklahoma was snapped up. Oklahoma City and other towns were established in a matter of hours. Cowboy Evan Barnard, who

THE LAND RUSH OF 1889

Arthur Dunham, a teenaged railroad worker, watched the first Oklahoma land rush:

> I stood on a box car along side the depot at the zero hour of 12 o'clock noon. My astonishment was complete—people seemed to spring up as if by magic as far as the eye could reach. I could see them racing in every direction, some on horses, some in vehicles, and a greater number on foot. They were carrying all sorts of impedimenta—some had spades, some stakes, some clothing, some had hand-bags, some had pots and pans, or other cooking utensils. My words are not adequate to describe the scene. I then commenced to realize that history was in the making.

During the 1889 land rush, newly arrived settlers protect the town lots they have staked out. In a matter of days, the town of Guthrie would rise on this site.

had worked in Indian Territory before the land rush, was there. The night after the great rush, he recalled, "lights flickered all over the country from the campfires of the settlers. It was a great change for the cowpunchers to see the great cattle country transferred in a day from a region with thousands of cattle to one with thousands of people moving about. We wondered what they would do to make a living."

Barnard was right to wonder. Many of these settlers, and those who joined the land rushes that followed, were ill prepared to make an Oklahoma farm succeed. For every successful farm there were abandoned claims; for every growing town there was a ghost town or an exhausted community struggling against harsh conditions it hadn't

A decade after the first land rush, 40 percent of Oklahoma's farmers were sharecroppers. A decade later, a third of the state's farm population had to move from one farm to another in search of work—a far cry from the hopes for a prosperous, independent living that brought so many of them to Oklahoma in the first place.

foreseen. The rush for Oklahoma land was matched by a quiet retreat of broken hopes.

The land that settlers abandoned often wound up in the hands of big landlords. As new waves of poor farmers arrived to pursue the Oklahoma dream they found little land to own, but plenty to rent.

By the early twentieth century, tenant farming, or "sharecropping," was bigger in Oklahoma than in any other state. Landlords would let sharecroppers till the soil in exchange for a portion of the crop they grew. Sharecroppers never got rich on the deal. Most years, they counted themselves lucky to survive.

STATEHOOD AND OIL

By 1906, all the land that had once been held in common by the tribes of Indian Territory had been divided among individuals—tribal members and non-Indian newcomers. So many new settlers had arrived that only one in ten residents were Indian. The next

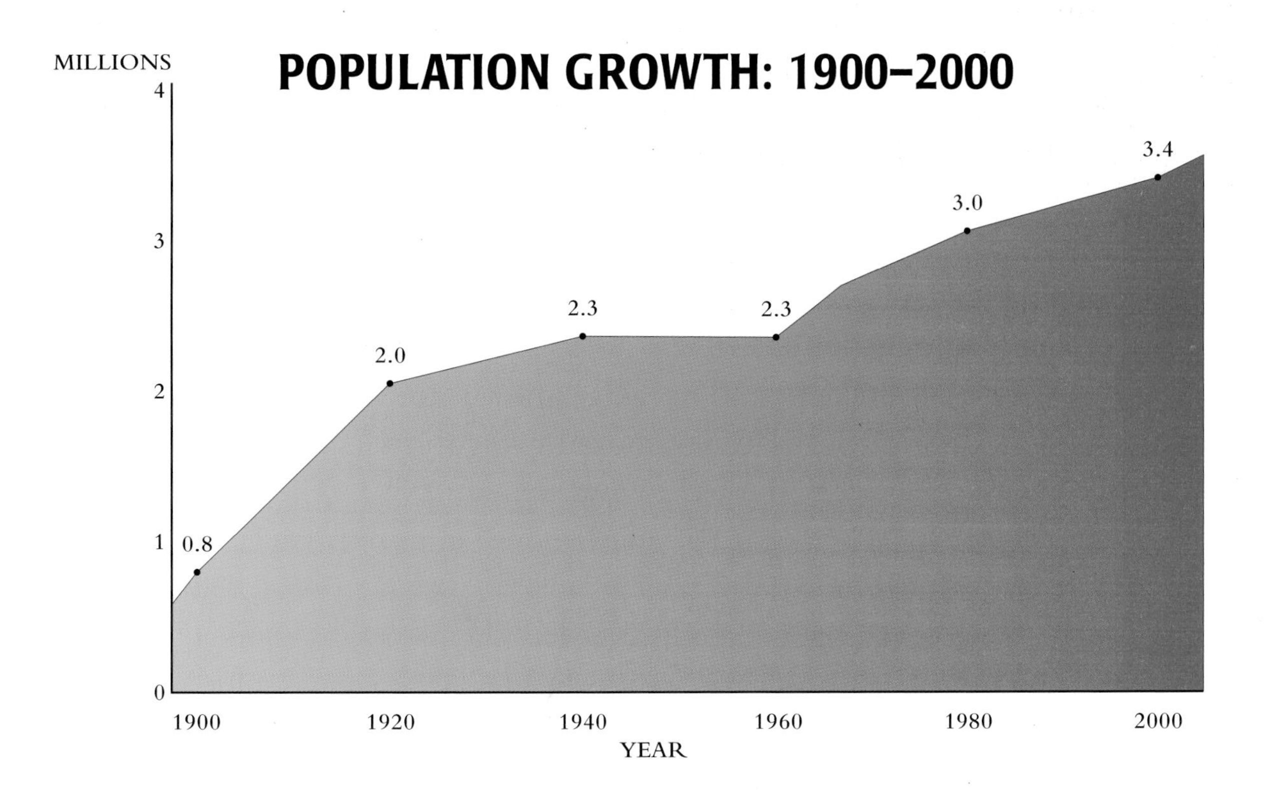

year, Congress voted to make Oklahoma the forty-sixth state.

A lot of newcomers were attracted not by land but by Oklahoma's new boom industry: petroleum. Beneath the newest American state lay fantastic amounts of oil and gas. New inventions such as the automobile boosted demand for oil, and new technologies made collecting and selling it highly profitable.

The change in the air was apparent to visitors such as German sociologist Max Weber, who wrote in 1905, "There is a fabulous bustle here, and I cannot help but find tremendous fascination in it, despite the stench of petroleum and the fumes." Oil put Oklahoma on the economic map. Folksinger Woody Guthrie put it this way: "Oil was more than gold ever was or will be, because you can't make any hair salve or perfume, TNT, or roofing material or drive a car with just gold. You can't pipe that gold back East and run them big factories, either."

Oklahoma City grew around its own oil fields during the boom years. "City Well Hurls 'Liquid Gold' High Over Oil Derrick," announced a 1928 headline. Soon, hundreds of wells were tapping the city's oil field, which was one of the nation's largest producers during the 1930s.

Besides oil, Oklahoma became known for melodramatic politics. The state legislature removed two governors from office for offenses that seemed trivial to outsiders. In 1930, "Alfalfa" Bill Murray won the job. Murray became famous for his shabby clothes, unkempt moustache, and tirades against bankers and oil barons. Some thought Murray undignified; others championed him as the "common man governor." Either way, his behavior caught nationwide attention.

OIL'S BLOODY UNDERSIDE

Tulsa grew on the strength of the oil boom. The diversity and promise of urban life, however, also contained the seeds of racial intolerance. On one vicious day in 1921, Tulsa fell into chaos. A white lynch mob threatened to kill a black man falsely accused of assaulting a white woman. A group of armed blacks confronted the mob. The conflict exploded into a day of brutal violence in which as many as three hundred African Americans may have died. Gunfire and fire-bombings all but leveled the Greenwood neighborhood where most black Tulsans lived. The riot "may have been the worst incident of racial violence in American history," says writer Scott Ellsworth.

Kinney Booker, eight years old at the time, remembered a narrow escape after white rioters set his family's house ablaze. "At first, I hated all white people," he admitted. He recalled, though, that a white family sheltered his after the riot.

Booker, like most other Tulsans, tried hard to forget the terrible event. Schoolchildren rarely heard it discussed in class. In 1997, though, the Oklahoma state legislature formed the Tulsa Race Riot Commission to investigate and set the record straight. Oklahoma schoolchildren now use the Tulsa Race Riot of 1921 as an opportunity to think about racial intolerance.

Oklahoma City's first successful oil well blew a gusher in 1928 whose roar could be heard for miles. It marked the discovery of one of the world's major oil fields and the emergence of petroleum as a major part of Oklahoma's economy.

DEPRESSION, DROUGHT, AND DUST BOWL

Stock crashes. Job losses. Bank failures. Hunger. Desperation. The Great Depression affected every American in the 1930s, but it may have hit Oklahomans hardest. Like other Americans, they confronted a wrecked economy, but they also endured the Dust Bowl. Western Oklahoma was at the heart of the area where drought, high winds, and plow-damaged fields combined to create disaster in the 1930s. Storms lifted the ravaged soil from the fields and hurled it through the air, burying some farms to the rooftops and leaving others surrounded by scoured wastelands.

A third of a million Oklahomans, mostly poor sharecroppers from the western plains, abandoned the state during the 1930s to seek a livelihood somewhere else. Many found after hard traveling that work was just as scarce elsewhere, and decent treatment scarcer. Wherever they went, the Dust Bowl migrants were both

A dust storm in Cimarron County. Karen Hesse's tiny poem "Broken Promise" sums up the Oklahoma Dust Bowl with perfect austerity:

It rained
a little
everywhere
but here.

pitied and feared. Whether they came from Oklahoma or other hard-hit states such as Texas or Kansas, they were called "Okies." The migrants learned that the word meant poor, stupid, dirty, and desperate. Over time, though, the shame associated with the word shifted to pride. Like the sooners, the Okies became heroes of Oklahoma folklore.

WAR, PEACE, AND PROSPERITY

As suddenly as the Great Depression and the Dust Bowl had knocked Oklahoma to pieces, World War II helped put it back together. Even before the United States entered World War II in 1941, Oklahoma was building Tinker Air Force Base near Oklahoma City. With the expansion of Vance Air Force Base near Enid and Fort Sill Military Reservation near Lawton, Oklahoma became home to some of the most important military bases in the country. Thousands of soldiers trained at Oklahoma bases during the war. The state distinguished itself in combat as well. Oklahomans in the Forty-fifth Infantry division, many of them Indians, fought valiantly in Europe. "Your division is one of the best, if not the best division in the history of American armies," General George Patton told them.

James Smith of Okemah served in the Forty-fifth. "Lots of men died. Lots of men were wounded. But we made it, by God. We had initiative, and we knew we had to do some real bold fighting," he recalled. "So we got it all together and got the job done. Just a bunch of hard-core Okies."

Memories of the depression, the Dust Bowl, and wartime sacrifice began to fade in the decades following the war. For once, the state's history became relatively dull—and Oklahomans liked it that way. Agriculture, oil, and the military provided a diversified economy that brought prosperity to most Oklahomans. More recently, telecommunications, food distribution, and other service industries have rounded out the state's economy.

Just as the term *Okies* had pinned Dust Bowl desperation to the state, the Broadway play *Oklahoma!* and the movie that followed remade that image in the 1950s. After watching the rousing musical, Americans thought of Oklahoma as a backdrop for cowboys and romance, "where the corn grows high as an elephant's eye." But all the while, the state was growing more urban and its economy more sophisticated. As Oklahoma moves forward, it continues to surprise.

Tinker Air Force Base near Lawton was built in a hurry to support the armed forces during World War II. This massive repair hangar prepared planes for overseas campaigns.

3 DEMOCRACY IN THE RAW

The capitol in Oklahoma City

ATE OF OKLAHOMA

"No other place in the world offers a more gruesome study of democracy in the raw—nor of how thoroughly it can be cooked," Oklahoman George Milburn wrote a half-century ago about his state. True, Oklahoma's early politics were often chaotic and colorful. But today the state has a government that suits the majority's desire for conservatism and low taxes, one that stays out of most aspects of daily life. You might say it's "democracy on a diet."

INSIDE GOVERNMENT

Some of the biggest decisions affecting Oklahoma are made by the federal government in Washington, D.C. But other important laws affecting everyday life are made, enforced, and interpreted by the state government.

The constitution of Oklahoma divides the work among three branches of government: legislative, executive, and judicial.

Legislative. The legislature (the 48-member senate and the 101-member house of representatives) is the lawmaking part of state government. The legislature meets every year to debate proposals for new laws. If both houses vote for a proposal it is sent to the governor, whose approval makes it law. Representatives are elected to two-year terms and senators to four-year terms.

Executive. The governor, the "chief executive," is chosen in a

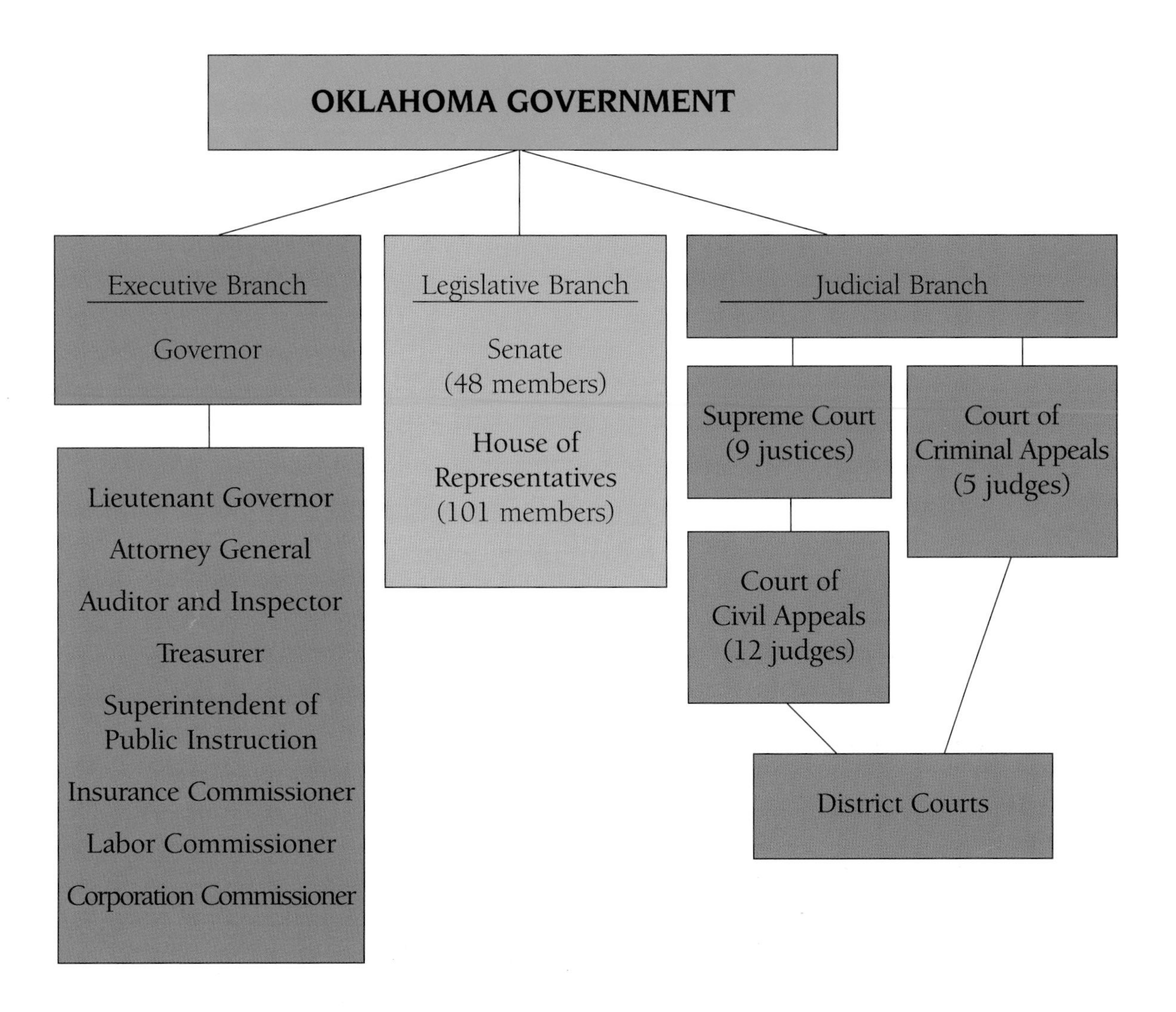

statewide election every four years. Other elected executive officials include the lieutenant governor and the attorney general.

The governor oversees the operation of the departments and agencies that make up the rest of the executive branch. These include the department of corrections, which operates the jails and prisons; the department of education, which oversees the schools; and the department of public safety, which issues driver's licenses and manages the Oklahoma Highway Patrol. These departments and others are designed to carry out laws passed by the legislature—making sure that prison and school cafeterias don't serve spoiled food, for example, and catching drivers who break traffic laws. The governor also works with the legislature to decide which political issues will be considered every year, and either signs their proposals into law or rejects—vetoes—them. The legislature has the final say, however, for it can override a governor's veto with the approval of two-thirds of the members of each house.

Judicial. The judicial branch is the part of state government that interprets state law. Judges help decide whether those accused of breaking the law are guilty or innocent. They also consider whether the legislature's decisions and the actions of the executive branch agree with the laws and constitution of Oklahoma.

The backbone of Oklahoma's judicial branch is its system of district courts, which hear cases in twenty-six districts around the state. Above these are the courts of criminal and civil appeals, where disputed rulings from the district courts are reviewed. If there are further disputes in a civil case, the supreme court can review it, but unlike in most states, Oklahoma's supreme court does not review criminal cases. The court, which has nine justices appointed by the governor and approved by the legislature, does however have some management responsibilities over the court of criminal appeals.

TRIBAL GOVERNMENT

The cities and counties of every state have governments, too. But nowhere else are there as many tribal governments as in Oklahoma.

Thirty-nine Indian tribes have headquarters there—far more than in any other state.

Indians are full citizens of the United States and of Oklahoma, and many have been leaders in government. (In fact, five of the eleven Indians who have served in the U.S. Congress represented Oklahoma.) However, Indians who are enrolled members of a tribe have rights and responsibilities under the tribe's government, too.

Although each tribe does things a little differently, most have adopted a three-branch government similar to Oklahoma's. A typical tribe elects a chief as executive and a tribal council as legislature, and maintains a tribal court system. A tribe's court system, not

Wallace Coffey made improving schools a top priority during his time as tribal chairman for the Comanche Tribes of Oklahoma.

Oklahoma's, has jurisdiction over certain crimes and disputes, especially when they occur on Indian land or when a dispute is among tribal members.

TOUGH ON CRIME

Oklahoma locks up a lot of people. About 1 of every 160 Oklahomans call a jail or prison cell home. Only Texas and Louisiana have higher rates of imprisonment. Part of the reason for this is that lawbreakers get longer jail sentences than they would receive in many other states.

The state also condemns more criminals to death than many other states, and most of its residents strongly support the death penalty. Stephen Wood, who was executed for murder in 1998, was no exception. "Just because it's me . . . my feelings haven't changed," he told a judge. "As a matter of fact, it's strengthened them."

Children learn that crime doesn't pay, too. Judge Richard Clarke sometimes conducts trials in schools to give students a taste of how lawbreakers are punished. "I would never want to experience what these people had to," said high school student Brandon Harris after watching the judge sentence three drunk drivers to jail in his school lunchroom. "I would never do it."

DIRECT DEMOCRACY

Oklahoma is one of just three states—New Mexico and Louisiana are the others—that allow what most Americans consider a grue-

A LONELY STAND AGAINST DEATH

Standing apart from most Oklahomans is Bud Welch, whose daughter Julie died when the Murrah Federal Building in Oklahoma City was bombed in 1995. "When I first spoke out against the death penalty, I was a freak," the gas station owner recalls. "To me, it's so simple. We're not teaching our young people right from wrong" when criminals are executed. "I don't know why people struggle with it so much."

Welch feels enraged by his daughter's death, but he fought hard to spare convicted bombers Timothy McVeigh and Terry Nichols the death penalty. "It wasn't going to bring Julie back. It was all about revenge. It was all about hate." Welch told McVeigh's sister, "I don't want your brother to die, and I'll do everything I can do to make sure that doesn't happen."

Bud Welch's efforts were not enough: McVeigh was condemned to die. On the day of his sentencing, about forty members of the victims' families gathered at the site of the bombing. Kevin Acers remembers seeing Welch "about five feet outside of that circle, standing completely alone because they were waiting to cheer the announcement of the decision for death.

"And no one was standing with Bud."

some sport: cockfighting. But many Oklahomans oppose the sport, which pits chickens with razor-sharp "slashers" and "gaffs" attached to their feet in bloody fights, usually to the death.

"Cockfighting is really a sickness in our society," claims Gary Moore, a Tulsan involved in the effort to ban it in Oklahoma. But cockfighting opponents have never convinced the state legislature to do away with it. Recently, they turned to another strategy:

When its legs are fitted with curved blades called gaffs, a cockerel like this is ready to fight to the death in a cockfight. Oklahoma is one of the last states in which this sport is legal.

placing an anti-cockfighting initiative on the election ballot so that voters can decide the issue directly.

Oklahoma has long had some of the most liberal direct democracy laws in the nation. These laws allow citizens to decide a question directly. To place an initiative on the ballot, a group must collect the signatures of 8 percent of the state's voters. Then the question goes directly to the voters, whose decision becomes law no matter what the legislature and the governor wish.

If the cockfighting question gets on the ballot, people on both sides of the issue will work to sway the voters to their side. Cockfighters are ready for the battle. "I like these birds because they have the same attitude as me," claims cockfighter Sharon McFarland. "Don't tell me 'no.' It makes me madder-n-hell. They're independent. Proud."

A CHANGING ECONOMY

Oklahoma's economy was once dominated by farming and oil, but now it relies more on service industries and manufacturing. Typical of the change is Tulsa's Williams Corporation. It has installed fiberoptic cables along its natural gas pipelines, adding telecommunications to an old energy network. Oklahoma City's Fleming, Inc. is a major grocery supplier to some of the nation's largest supermarkets. Other companies maintain airplanes, rent cars, sell paper products, and install computer systems—all service businesses that have taken the state by storm.

Tulsa is a center for petroleum production and research—only the Texas cities of Houston and Dallas have larger roles in the oil industry.

GROSS STATE PRODUCT: $82 BILLION

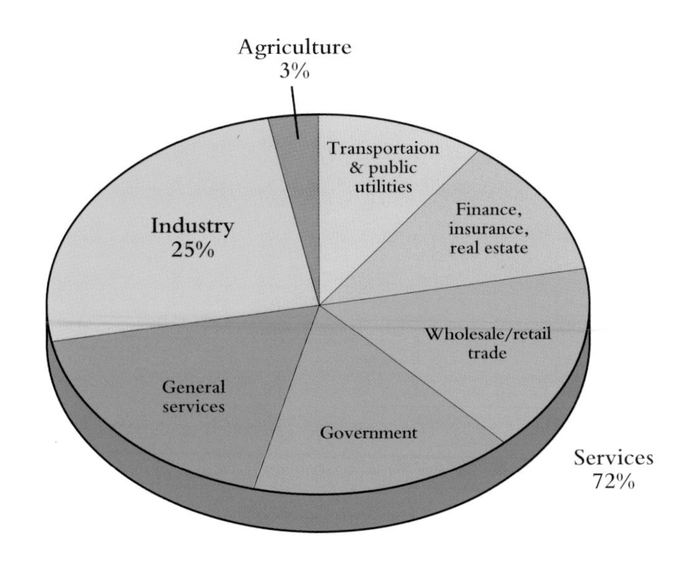

(2000 estimated)

Williams and Fleming are major corporations, but much of Oklahoma's economic strength comes from small businesses. Sixty-year-old Edith Williams, for example, runs a tree-trimming service in Shawnee. "She can outwork any man I know, even those half her age," says an employee. Since thousands of small businesses flourish in Oklahoma, that kind of hard work amounts to a major slice of the state's economy.

DOWN ON THE FARM

Though agriculture is not as large a part of Oklahoma's economy as it used to be, farmers still play an important role, especially in rural

Crickett Garcia builds fancy cowboy boots at his shop in Guthrie. Small businesses such as his are the backbone of Oklahoma's economy.

EARNING A LIVING

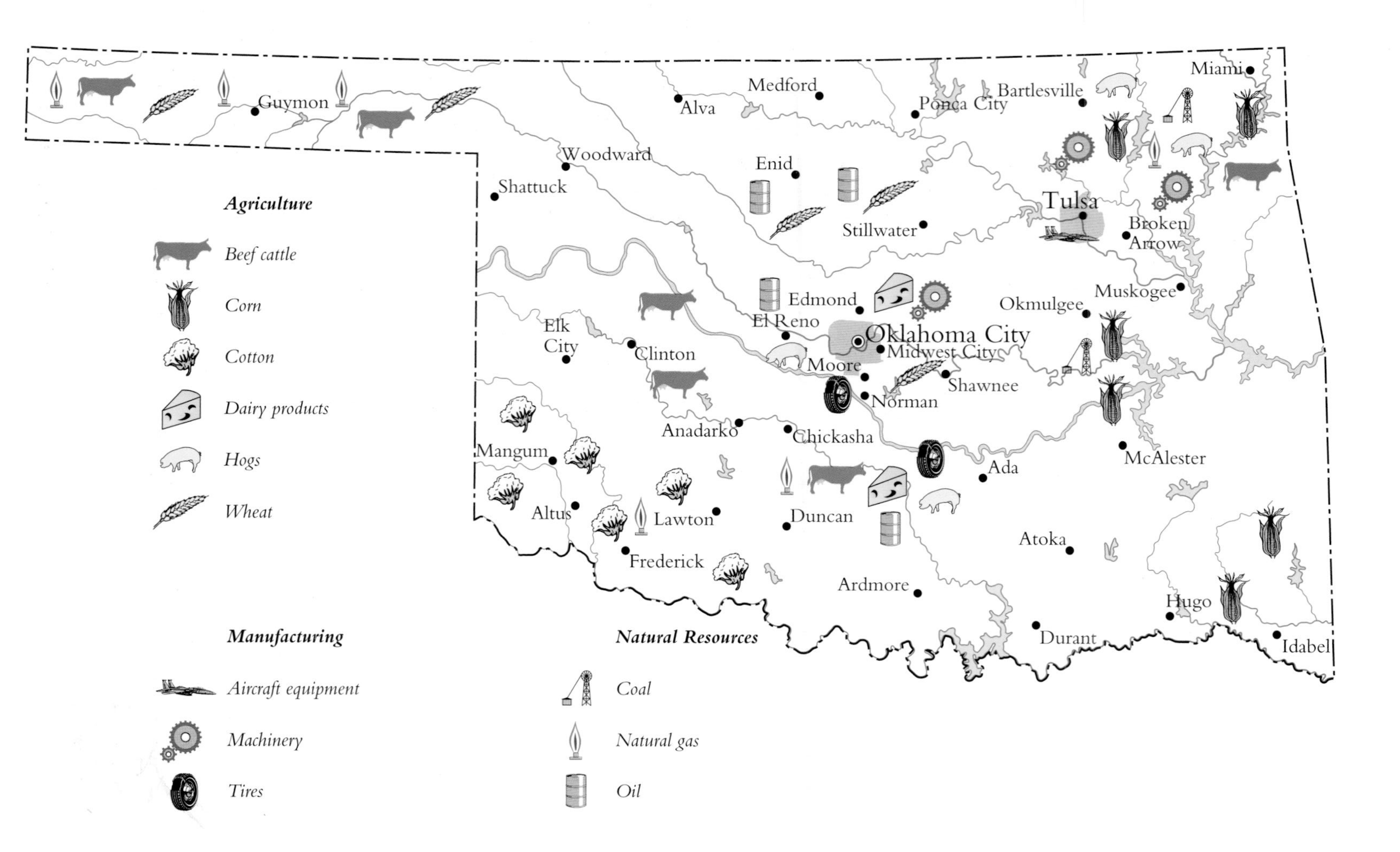

Potatoes thrive in cool weather, so Oklahomans plant them early for harvest in the late spring.

areas. "If they don't make money, we don't make money," explains Cheryl McKelvy, a waitress at Rhonda's Cafe in Snyder.

Even during good years, farming is tough work. "Everything you see out there's made out of sweat," farmer Ned DeWitt once wrote. "I know to the penny what I had to pay for them pigs and horses and chickens. . . . and I know what they'll bring on the market right

SWINE FACTORIES

Is Oklahoma becoming "the swine state"? Hog production increased tenfold during the 1990s because gigantic "factory" hog farms have opened in the state. In 1992, Seaboard Farms started an enormous hog-raising enterprise in the Panhandle. The company has its own meatpacking plant where hogs are slaughtered and processed into pork chops and bacon.

Some boast that "swine factories" such as these help the state's rural economy. Over 2,400 people work at the Seaboard plant, for example. But most came from outside the area. "We've brought in immigrants to work, because we can't get local workers," says Rick Hoffman of Seaboard. Locals say the jobs are lousy, and remember that their county had little unemployment before Seaboard arrived.

People living near the new farms worry about another problem: the odor. The factory farms pour hog waste into big, smelly ponds. Earl Mitchell, who raises pigs on a small Panhandle farm, insists that pig farms don't stink if they're not gigantic. "We've had many friends who say they hardly smell our pigs," he says.

The biggest impact is on smaller hog farmers such as Mitchell, who is quitting because he can't afford to compete with the factory farms. Meatpackers pay as little as twenty dollars for pigs raised on small farms—too low for them to make a profit. "Megafarms" raise hogs more cheaply and sell them for more money because meat-packers will pay extra for a promise to supply millions of pigs.

now, because I've had to put out too much hard work not to know."

Oklahoma is one of the biggest producers of hard winter wheat, the kind used to make bread. Wheat prices have fallen in recent years, though. Cotton, once the mainstay of Oklahoma agriculture, has suffered a similar decline. What's left? "Peanuts, it's the only thing we've got left out here," answers Brian Silk, who farms near Delhi. "We just want fair, market prices. Peanuts are the fairest thing we've got right now." Growing a greater variety of crops that can

Farmer Darrell Coble and his sons grow wheat, Oklahoma's most important crop by far. The state grows more than half a billion dollars worth of the grain every year—seven times what cotton, the state's second most valuable crop, brings in.

endure Oklahoma's weird weather may help Oklahoma's farmers in the long run.

UNDER THE DERRICK

Even more than agriculture, Oklahoma's energy industry has suffered in recent years. In the 1970s, the state's energy industry boomed—supply was low and demand was high, so prices were high. But by the

Despite the seesaw of oil prices, Oklahoma's petroleum industry continues to be a vital part of its economy.

1990s, the situation had reversed. Oil prices dropped far below the cost of production for many Oklahoma wells—to as little as six dollars a barrel (less than the cost of the barrel itself!). "The average stripper well in Oklahoma needs about $11 per barrel as a break-even," said Jim Palm, former head of the Oklahoma Independent Petroleum Association. His group predicted that three-quarters of the state's 90,000 oil wells might close down for good unless prices rise significantly in years to come.

If they don't, it will be a blow, but it won't be the disaster it once would have been. Oklahoma's diversified economy means that other areas will flourish if energy or agriculture slides. Cheap gasoline will fuel automobiles rented by Oklahomans; cheap wheat will boost grocery orders filled by Oklahoma corporations. Working together in a variety of pursuits, Oklahomans are better prepared to face the changing economy.

4 A CHORUS OF CULTURES

Most states belong to a single region, but Oklahoma is different. It's a rare place where several regions collide: the Midwest, the South, and the West. Overlapping these regional identities is the rich variety of cultures that dozens of Indian tribes have brought to the state.

REGIONAL CROSSROADS

As a result, Oklahoma has one of the richest and most complicated cultures of all the states. There's a long-standing split between urban and rural. Indian areas contrast with those dominated by whites. A few nearly all–African-American towns founded after the Civil War remain vital today.

Northern and southern culture mix along a division that roughly follows the Canadian River across the middle of the state. Many settlers in northern Oklahoma came from midwestern states such as Kansas. Southern Oklahoma, by contrast, was peopled by migrants from southern states such as Texas and Arkansas. Those settlers brought cultural styles that persist today. Grain elevators tower over northern towns such as Alva and Perry, which have a steak-and-potatoes feel. Cotton wagons rumble through southern towns such as Durant and Hugo; they have a barbecue-and-cornbread attitude.

At the same time, most Oklahomans share a western sensibility.

Spectators take in an event during the Chuck Wagon Gathering and Children's Cowboy Festival at Oklahoma City's National Cowboy Hall of Fame.

Only Texans own more horses, and Oklahoma City is home to one of the largest cattle markets in the world.

Few Oklahomans really have much to do with horses, cattle, and ranches today. It's a bit of a mystery why they remain so fond of cowboy culture. Maybe they relate to the Oklahomans who were famous movie cowboys, such as Will Rogers and Gene Autry. Oklahoma City is home to the National Cowboy Hall of Fame, and many of the state's museums specialize in western and Indian art. A number of towns hold rodeos. Kids identify with country music stars such as Oklahoma's own Garth Brooks more than in many other parts of the country.

RURAL OKLAHOMA

Though most Oklahomans live in cities, rural life is what residents and outsiders alike usually think of when they picture the state. Oklahoma doesn't call to mind city skylines as much as soft green crops of winter wheat broken by patches of bright red dirt.

Many Oklahoma kids are active in a classic rural club, the Future Farmers of America (FFA). They learn the skills and rewards of an agricultural career and travel to events that the club sponsors. "We've seen a whole lot more country than other kids in our school," Jamie Hix boasts. Some of the organization's meetings draw in whole communities. "Everybody in town baked pies," recounted Melissa Davis, a teenager from Oaks. "There were 400 to 500 pies" at the state FFA convention she attended.

NATIVE AMERICA

You can learn from license plates. Oklahoma's boast that it is "Native America." "Both insiders and outsiders associate Indians with Oklahoma," notes anthropologist Luke Lassiter. "Marketing Indians is big business."

There's a reality underneath the image. More than a quarter million Indians live in Oklahoma, more than in any state besides California. Eight percent of Oklahomans are Indians, a higher percentage than any state besides Alaska and New Mexico. Depending on who's counting, up to sixty-seven different tribes are represented—by far the largest number of different native cultures in any state.

Oklahoma's Indians struggle to preserve cultural traditions. A Creek day-care and cultural center in Okmulgee brings in storytellers and artists and serves kids Creek foods such as fry bread and wild grape dumplings. The center takes pains to teach young children Creek, which like many Indian languages is in danger of dying out. The focus on children is important, according to Creek chief Perry Beaver: "You don't wait until they're 20 or 30" to build

Tepees join the skyline each year when the Red Earth Festival, the "World's Largest Powwow," returns to Oklahoma City.

an interest in native culture. Alexis Crosley, the father of a child who attends the center, agrees. "I don't know how to speak Creek," he admits. "I want my kids to know all of that."

Oklahoma's Indians, like those elsewhere, struggle to convey their traditional culture to new generations. "I never did learn how to speak Kiowa and my grandfather could only speak a little broken English," recalls lawyer Ethel Krepps. "However, we didn't let that stand in our way. We would sit next to each other and hold hands. . . . We never knew what the other was talking about but it didn't really matter. We knew what we were trying to tell each other."

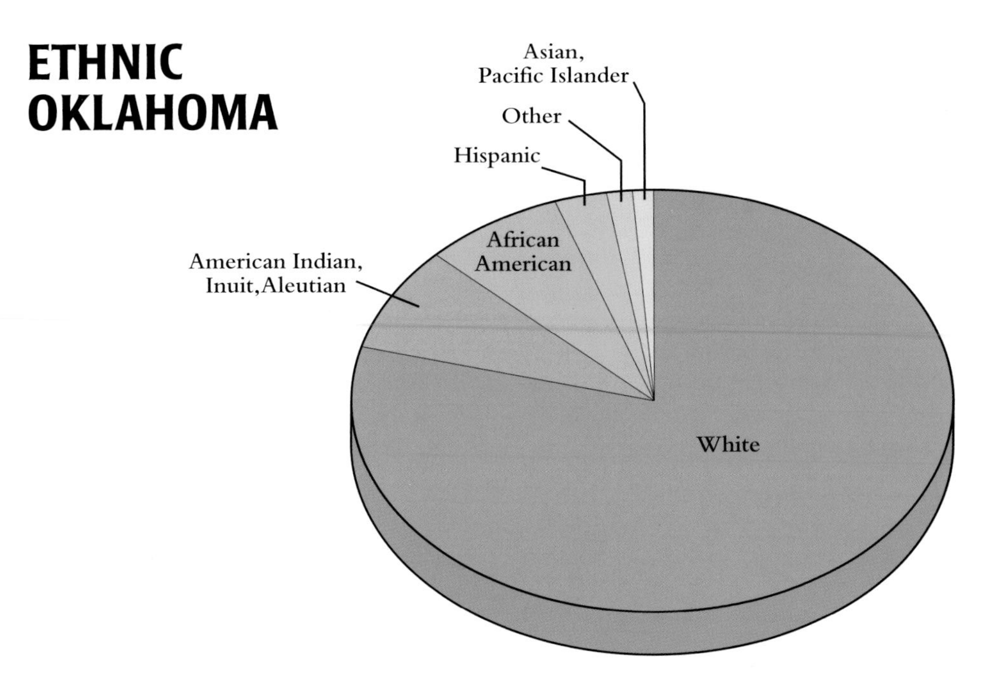

POWWOWS

Perhaps the best example of Indians working together to preserve their heritage is the powwow. Summer is "powwow season" in Oklahoma, with events scheduled for every weekend all over the state.

Powwows combine dance, song, camaraderie, and the celebration of tradition. Each powwow is unique, but all have common features and a common origin. Not long ago, the famous Osage ballerina Maria Tallchief remembers, Indians "were subject to government edicts which were designed to destroy tribal customs." Quietly, Indians preserved old ceremonies and invented new traditions. "We didn't know it then," says Jerry Bread, "but these social gatherings were to evolve into what today is called a powwow." Oklahoma, with its complex mix of Indian cultures, has led

THE FORTUNATE HUNTER

Folktales aren't always serious. Many Indian legends are intended to make people laugh. This tall tale was told by an elderly Cherokee storyteller, Gahnô, many years ago.

A hunter had been sick for a long time. Finally he felt well, but also very hungry. He went into the woods to hunt.

The hunter spied a deer standing across a stream. He took aim and shot. His arrow pierced the deer's neck and pinned its quivering body to the trunk of a tree.

The hunter squatted to remove his boots so he could cross the stream. He felt something wriggling underneath him, and found that he was sitting on a rabbit. The rabbit was dying, so he grabbed it and struck it against the ground to finish it off. The rabbit whacked a sleeping family of quails and killed them all, too.

The hunter crossed the stream, his boots trailing in the water. When he tried to put them on, he found that they were brimming with glistening, flopping fish.

The hunter yanked the arrow to free the deer's body. From the arrow hole gushed honey—a beehive was hidden in a hollow of the tree.

The hunter collected the deer, rabbit, quails, fish, and honey, and hauled them home. He was still hungry, but life was going to be good now!

Participants at the Red Earth Festival come for the feeling of friendship and community that is at the heart of each event. "How many times do you actually have something to acknowledge that friendship?" asks powwow participant Haddon Nauni. The powwow "teaches respect for one another. Strengthens the bond."

the country in developing the modern powwow. The "World's Biggest Powwow" is part of Oklahoma City's Red Earth Festival, which draws participants from more than one hundred tribes.

Song is one basic element of the powwow. "From ancient times the people have sung in times of trouble and danger, to cure the sick, to confound their enemies," explains Jimalee Burton, a Cherokee. Powwows help to preserve those traditions, as a Kiowa song by Leonard Cozad demonstrates:

> Where are the old people?
> The *Kiowa* people?
> The *songs* are the only things we have left, *now.*
> All the old people went somewhere,
> they're *gone.*
> And all we've got left now are these songs,
> to *sing.*

Also basic to every powwow is dancing. A typical powwow features several long dances spread out over a couple of days. "Powwow dancers are athletes," says Darrell Wildcat, a member of the Euchee and Kiowa tribes. "Many dances, especially the women's Fancy Shawl and the Fancy War Dance, require tremendous strength and stamina."

BLACK TOWNS ON THE PRAIRIE

Oklahoma's varied culture also features a handful of mostly black towns founded by former slaves after the Civil War. Unlike freed slaves elsewhere, many in Indian Territory gained allotments of land as the Indian tribal lands were carved up. That allowed them to found almost thirty black towns, more than were established in all the other the states combined. Residents of these towns enjoyed real power over their communities at a time when most African Americans were excluded from politics and other aspects of public life.

Only thirteen of these towns remain today, and many of them are shrinking. "The Great Depression . . . was devastating to the all-black towns," says historian Curry Ballard. Residents left to find

A parader at the annual Boley rodeo. Founded by freed slaves in 1903, Boley was once the largest predominantly black town in the United States.

economic opportunities elsewhere, and few returned. Boley is one that looks to endure. This town of fewer than 1,000 residents swells to 15,000 every Memorial Day weekend when it hosts the Boley rodeo, an event that also features barbecue, music, and a parade.

CELEBRATING TOGETHER

The Oklahoma State Fair, held every fall in Tulsa, is a big party featuring events and exhibits from every corner of the state. Some are traditional, such as livestock judging and midway rides. Others aren't—such as Sharon BuMann's sculpture of a cow and two children, which was displayed in a big glass refrigerator. It would have melted otherwise, for it was made of half a ton of butter. "I always told my children never to play with their food," BuMann admits. Fairgoers enjoy odd treats that reappear every year, such as pork chop sand-wiches and fried pickles.

Almost every town seems to hold some kind of festival, and many of them have food themes. You could eat your way across Oklahoma, celebrating chili in Tulsa, strawberries in Stilwell, huck-leberries in Jay, watermelons in Rush Springs, and cheese in Watonga. El Reno celebrates Fried Onion Burger Day, and Vinita offers the World's Largest Calf Fry Festival and Cook-Off. For dessert, there's Okmulgee's Pecan Festival, Wewoka's Sorghum Day, and Erick's Honey Festival.

Some celebrations happen in many different cities across the state. An example is Juneteenth, the holiday marking the end of slavery after the Civil War. Towns from Tulsa to Enid to Ponca City observe it with parades, picnics, music, and games. Some celebra-

Whether it's the Strawberry Festival in Stilwell or the World Championship Hog Calling Contest in Weatherford, Oklahomans love community celebrations. "I've never been to a bad one," claims Sandy Pantlik of the Oklahoma Department of Tourism. "We have no shortage of creativity."

RECIPE: PANHANDLE COLESLAW

There's a lot of rotten coleslaw in this world: droopy, soggy, chewed up, or sweet as candy. But in Oklahoma they know how to make coleslaw right, and they'll serve it with almost any meal. It's incredibly easy to make—you won't even need the recipe after your second or third batch. Have an adult help you with the chopping.

1 green cabbage
2 carrots, scraped
2 tablespoons vinegar
1 tablespoon mayonnaise
1 teaspoon sugar
1 teaspoon mustard
½ teaspoon caraway seeds (optional)
salt and pepper to taste

Peel the tough outer leaves off the cabbage and cut it in half. Working slowly and carefully with a sharp knife, shave off thin, lacy slices into a big bowl. (Half the crime of bad coleslaw is grinding it into tiny bits.) Grate the carrots into the same bowl.

In another bowl, combine the other ingredients to make the dressing. Mix thoroughly and pour it over the cabbage and carrots. Toss well, then refrigerate for a little while before serving.

Everyone makes coleslaw a little differently. Experiment until you have your own perfect recipe. Some "secret ingredients" to try: chopped peanuts, grated onions, crushed garlic, fresh lemon juice—or anything else that seems right to you.

Celebrations of Juneteenth take many forms. In Tulsa, the holiday also helps mark the memory of victims of the 1921 race riot, which all but destroyed the predominantly black Greenwood neighborhood.

tions are small affairs, often organized by church congregations. Others, such as Oklahoma City's, attract lots of participants. "This is not a black thing, not a white thing, but something all of Oklahoma City can be proud of," said Jeffrey Carolina, who helps organize the celebration there.

PRIDE IN COMMUNITY: THE OKLAHOMA CITY BOMBING

Nine o'clock A.M., April 19, 1995: Workers arrive at their offices at the Murrah Federal Building in downtown Oklahoma City, leaving their children at the building's day-care center. The day begins like any other.

Two minutes later, Oklahoma changes forever. "Everything is the blackest black you can imagine, and I don't hear any noise. But I can feel the force of the air carrying me, and I know I'm flying in the air. . . . I can hear the sound of those concrete floors collapsing on each other right around me," remembers lawyer Duane Miller. "When the floor noise stops, the only other thing I can hear is the sound of one man calling for help." A bomb had exploded, tearing the building apart. The nation's worst brush with modern terrorism left 149 adults and 19 children dead.

Within moments, countless Oklahomans were becoming heroes. Workers who staggered from the rubble returned to search for survivors. "With no hesitation they dived right back in after their friends and co-workers," recalled one local. As word of the catastrophe spread, more and more Oklahomans reacted with generosity and courage. An hour after the bombing, hundreds had already lined up to donate blood. The streets snarled with traffic jams as volunteers arrived to help in any way they could. "We Okies have always been kind of a family, you know, but never like this," said one of them. "I guess it's because we really need each other now."

Across the country, people were amazed by the grace of Oklahomans' response to the tragedy. "Acts of heroism, sacrifice, compassion, and dedication . . . were so numerous as to be almost commonplace," reported the *Daily Oklahoman*. They transformed "a monument to terror" into "the symbol of man's humanity to man," wrote Gerald Hibbs of Edmond.

Even as the wrecked building was pulled down, people gathered quietly to watch and to attach objects to the fence surrounding it: photographs, flags, teddy bears, and letters expressing their grief. Today, the bombsite has been transformed into a public memorial for the victims, and a small part of the fence remains intact. The memorial also includes a reflecting pool and a field filled with 168 stone chairs, one for each person killed in the bombing. It is a place to meditate on a senseless tragedy—and on the sensitive and generous spirit of the people of Oklahoma.

After the bombing of the Murrah Federal Building in Oklahoma City, thousands of Oklahomans placed objects and letters near the fence surrounding it to remember the victims.

5 PROUD TO BE AN OKIE

For such a young state, Oklahoma has produced an impressive number of leaders, notables, and stars. Whether performers or politicians, astronauts or writers, lifelong residents or long-gone migrants to other places, these exceptional people have one thing in common: their home state has shaped their careers and contributed to their successes. They're all "proud to be Okies."

A CIVIL RIGHTS LEADER

Everybody knows something about the civil rights struggle that ended segregation, or separation of the races, in states such as Oklahoma. But few know that Oklahoma City was the site of important early victories in that struggle, and fewer still know about Clara Luper, the schoolteacher who led them.

Clara Luper's challenges to segregation started early. She was the first African American at the University of Oklahoma to receive a master's degree in history, a subject she taught in Oklahoma City schools for forty-one years. She was also active in the National Association for the Advancement of Colored People (NAACP), a pioneering civil rights organization. In 1957, she chaperoned a trip to New York for kids in the NAACP Youth Council. Most of the kids had never traveled outside of Oklahoma before. They were astonished to see whites and blacks using the same restaurants,

Clara Luper in her first home, the classroom. For years, her second home was on the front lines of protests to win equal rights for African Americans.

bathrooms, and other public places. What was normal in other states was still unthinkable in segregated Oklahoma.

Back home in the Sooner State, the Youth Council kids decided that "the Sooner we get rid of segregation, the better off we'll be." Luper's eight-year-old daughter, Marilyn, suggested a children's sit-in demonstration. Many parents would have been horrified—but Clara Luper thought it was a great idea and decided to help. On

August 19, 1958, she and twelve black children took seats at the Katz Drug Store's lunch counter. "Thirteen Cokes, please," said Luper.

The Cokes didn't come. "In a matter of minutes, we were surrounded by policemen of all sizes, with all kinds of facial expressions," she recalls. "The whites that were seated at the counter got up, leaving their food unfinished on the table and emptied their hate terms into the air."

Luper showed up at the lunch counter the next day, and the next. More and more children joined her. They'd leave splattered with food, drink, and spit, their ears ringing with insults. But the protest was working. It forced Oklahomans of all colors to think about the injustice of segregation. Before long, the first hamburger was served to one of Luper's protesters. "Within that hamburger was the whole essence of democracy," she said.

Before segregation finally became illegal in 1964, Luper had been jailed twenty-six times for leading protests at whites-only establishments. By the time she retired from teaching high school in 1989, her own experiences had become part of her students' history lessons. "She's taught us so much," said Steve Smith, one of her last students. "I know her legacy will live on."

CHEROKEE CHIEF

Most states' political leaders have made their contributions in local, state, or national government. In Oklahoma, they're just as likely to have made their marks in the governments of the state's Indian tribes. One remarkable leader is Wilma Mankiller, who was principal

OKLAHOMA WRITERS

Oklahoma has long inspired people to express themselves in the written word. Daniel Boorstin and John Hope Franklin, two highly regarded historians, got their starts in Oklahoma. Novelist Ralph Ellison is Oklahoma's most famous writer. His *Invisible Man* helped Americans confront racial intolerance during the 1950s and 1960s. It has been rated among the top twenty English-language novels of the twentieth century.

Wilma McDaniel's Dust Bowl poems explore the power of words against the backdrop of Oklahoma's harsh landscape and history. Here's one:

The Interpreter

Newly moved to Big Muddy
pretty girl
big for twelve

and I didn't know that Molly
couldn't read the newspapers
on our sharecrop walls

until she pointed at Gary Cooper
and asked me
What do they say about him
ain't he good looking

chief of the Cherokee Nation during a period of big challenges and important accomplishments.

Mankiller was born in Stilwell in 1945, the sixth of eleven children.

When Bill Clinton presented Wilma Mankiller with the Presidential Medal of Freedom for her leadership of the Cherokee Nation, she remarked, "It's kind of interesting to receive an award for something you love doing. It's like giving a bird an award for singing."

When she was eleven years old, her family moved to San Francisco, where Mankiller found teachers, friends, and a set of lifelong commitments. When protesters took over Alcatraz Island to fight for Indian rights, Mankiller was there to organize support. "If there was something going on, I was in the thick of it," she remembers.

After earning a degree in social work, Mankiller decided she was most interested in helping poor, rural Indians, so she went home to Oklahoma. She got big things done, and people noticed. Cherokee chief Ross Swimmer said that if Mankiller was leading a project, "it's not just a flash-in-the-pan idea . . . and she's not doing it for political reasons." When Swimmer resigned in 1985, Mankiller replaced him as principal chief, becoming the first woman to lead a major Indian tribe. Some Cherokees resisted the idea of a woman chief, but Mankiller won the tribe's confidence through strong leadership and good humor. Mankiller is "a nickname, and I earned it," she once joked to a male doubter.

Leading the country's second-largest Indian tribe was like being a state governor and a business executive at the same time—and at a troubled time. Many Cherokees lived in rural areas with few jobs and even fewer services such as health clinics and day-care. Mankiller helped the tribe fight these problems. "Poor people have a much greater capacity for leadership and for solving their own problems than they are ever given credit for," she declared. The size of the tribe tripled during her ten years as principal chief, as Cherokees who had drifted away from official tribal enrollment chose to return. The tribal budget doubled, which paid for new health centers and children's programs.

Mankiller fights hard for the Cherokee, but she also advocates the rights of all women across the nation. "Women my age, by and large, were not raised to be leaders," she points out. Her example was an inspiration to women, young and old, to challenge men for leadership positions in government and other places of power.

COWBOY SUPERSTAR

Today's celebrities often come from the world of television. In the early twentieth century, however, newspapers and radio produced superstars, as did the theater and the silent movie screen. The most versatile performer of that era was a part-Cherokee cowboy from Oklahoma named Will Rogers.

Rogers was born in Oologah, Indian Territory, in 1879. He grew up on his family's ranch and was a real cowboy before going off to play the part in a traveling Wild West show. He made his way to New York to perform rope tricks in vaudeville shows. After Rogers added humorous remarks to his act, people began paying

Will Rogers became a national star, but he never forgot his roots. "Oklahoma is the heart, it's the vital organ of our national existence," he boasted. Oklahomans were especially devastated when their favorite son lost his life in a plane crash in 1936.

more attention to the jokes than the lasso. Before long, people were packing the theater just to hear humor and comments on the day's news. He was a star.

Rogers soon added the movies to his list of accomplishments, becoming famous for playing folksy, homespun roles. But his greatest talent was with words, and his greatest fame came from his newspaper columns and radio broadcasts. By the late 1920s, millions of Americans read or listened to Rogers every day. "All I know is what I read in the papers," he'd often say—and then he'd go on to poke fun at world leaders, national politics, and current events. "Everything is funny as long as it is happening to somebody else," he'd conclude. His devoted audience agreed enthusiastically.

Though he never became a pilot, Will Rogers loved flying. In 1935, he and the famous Oklahoma aviator Wiley Post made a flying tour of Alaska. While struggling to take off, Post's plane crashed, killing both men instantly. The accident was front-page news for days. Flags flew at half-staff, and the entire country observed a moment of silence to honor one of America's first modern celebrities.

MUSICAL OKLAHOMA

Oklahoma has a rich musical heritage, from tribal songs to jazz to honky-tonk country. The pioneering jazz guitarist Charlie Christian built his career in Oklahoma City, as did Lester Young and Count Basie. Country music superstars Reba McEntire and Garth Brooks grew up in the state. The three brothers who make up the pop group Hanson are *still* growing up in Tulsa!

Woody Guthrie. "There is nothing sweet about Woody," said author John Steinbeck, "and there is nothing sweet about the songs he sings. But there is something more important for those who will listen. There is the will of the people to endure and fight against oppression. I think we call this the American spirit."

Far and away, though, the foremost musician of Oklahoma is Woody Guthrie. Guthrie was born in Okemah in 1912. "Ours was just another one of those little towns, I guess, about a thousand or more people, where everybody knows everybody else," he recalled. "On your way to the post office, you'd nod and speak to so many friends that your neck would be rubbed raw when you went in to get your mail if there was any."

Not all of Guthrie's childhood memories were fond. His family was torn apart by a series of tragedies, including his sister's death in a stove explosion and his mother's disintegrating health. By the time he was a young teenager, Guthrie was more or less on his own. He earned pennies singing on the streets of Okemah before beginning a life of travel.

Guthrie led a hobo's life for years, performing in migrant work camps and saloons. "I hate a song that makes you think that you are born to lose," he later said. "I am out to fight those kinds of songs to my very last breath of air and my last drop of blood." His songs depicting the hardships of the Great Depression and the Dust Bowl, such as "So Long, It's Been Good to Know You," were instant classics, and soon he was a star of American folk music.

"Woody was a rebel who didn't fit in," says music expert Guy Logsdon. "He was Oklahoma's most creative citizen. . . . He was interested in the everyday working person having a good time." Guthrie's life was cut tragically short by Huntington's chorea, the same disease that killed his mother. He spent the last fifteen years of his life in and out of hospitals as the disease robbed him of control over his movement and speech. It finally killed him in 1967.

Guthrie wrote more than a thousand songs, and his music has lived on. The British rocker Billy Bragg told an Okemah crowd celebrating Guthrie's eighty-sixth birthday that their native son was "one of the greatest lyrical poets that your country has produced this century." Guthrie has "not spoken his last words," Bragg said. Through his songs and the memory of his life, "He's still speaking to us."

OKIE IN SPACE

As the destination for displaced Indians and land rushers, and the starting point for Dust Bowl migrants, Oklahoma is certainly a state

Shannon Lucid aboard the Mir *space station. Five other Oklahomans have served as astronauts, including Thomas Stafford, who orbited the moon and commanded the first United States-Russian joint space mission in 1975.*

of travelers. There's absolutely no question which Oklahoman has journeyed farthest, though. That's astronaut Shannon Lucid, who holds the American record for time spent in space. During her record-breaking 1996 mission on Russia's *Mir* space station, she traveled an astonishing 75.2 million miles!

Lucid grew up in Bethany, Oklahoma. After earning a Ph.D. in biochemistry at the University of Oklahoma, she became one of the first six women chosen to train as a National Aeronautics and Space Administration (NASA) astronaut. Lucid made her first flight aboard a space shuttle in 1985. By the time she was selected for the *Mir* mission, she had already flown four times.

Lucid spent a year in Russia training for her mission aboard *Mir.* Aboard the space station, she managed a variety of experiments, including exploring the effects of weightlessness on animals and plants. One experiment had her growing wheat in an orbiting greenhouse. "It reminded me of Oklahoma," she said.

After five space flights, Lucid has spent 223 days in space—a world record for women, and an American record for all astronauts. She's not ready to hang up her space suit yet. "I guess I don't spend a lot of time looking back," she says. "I'm generally looking forward to a flight."

6 OKLAHOMA, OK!

Travelers to Oklahoma, prepare ahead! In some states, the attractions are all in a few places. In Oklahoma, they're spread from border to border in little hideaways that few people have heard of. Any single tour of Oklahoma is doomed to be incomplete, but here are some spots to visit for certain.

CHEROKEE COUNTRY

Northeastern Oklahoma is the most hospitable corner of the state in many ways. The land is green, rolling, and forested, and woven with lakes and streams. Its cities are the state's oldest, its history the most vivid.

Tahlequah is the capital of the Cherokee Nation. At its center is the Cherokee National Capitol, a handsome brick building completed in 1869. Near the capitol are the old Cherokee Supreme Court and the Cherokee National Prison. These buildings are as important for Cherokees as Washington, D.C., is for all Americans. Just out of town is the Cherokee Heritage Center, where a museum and a reproduction of a seventeenth-century Cherokee village are tucked within a dark pine forest. The tribe stages the Trail of Tears Drama most summers. It brings to life the sad story of their hard migration and resettlement in Indian Territory.

Nearby Muskogee, one of the oldest towns in Oklahoma, is today

The Cherokee Nation is the largest Indian tribe in Oklahoma. Its headquarters and cultural centers in and around Tahlequah preserve native culture for visitors and tribal members alike.

a spirited small city, the site of the Five Civilized Tribes Museum. Besides its historical collection, the museum hosts shows of contemporary Indian art and popular outdoor festivals where velvet ropes and glass cases don't get between visitors and tribal culture.

To the southeast, Spiro Mounds Archaeological State Park preserves the site of a major Indian religious and ceremonial center. Archaeologists have studied a dozen mounds spread over eighty

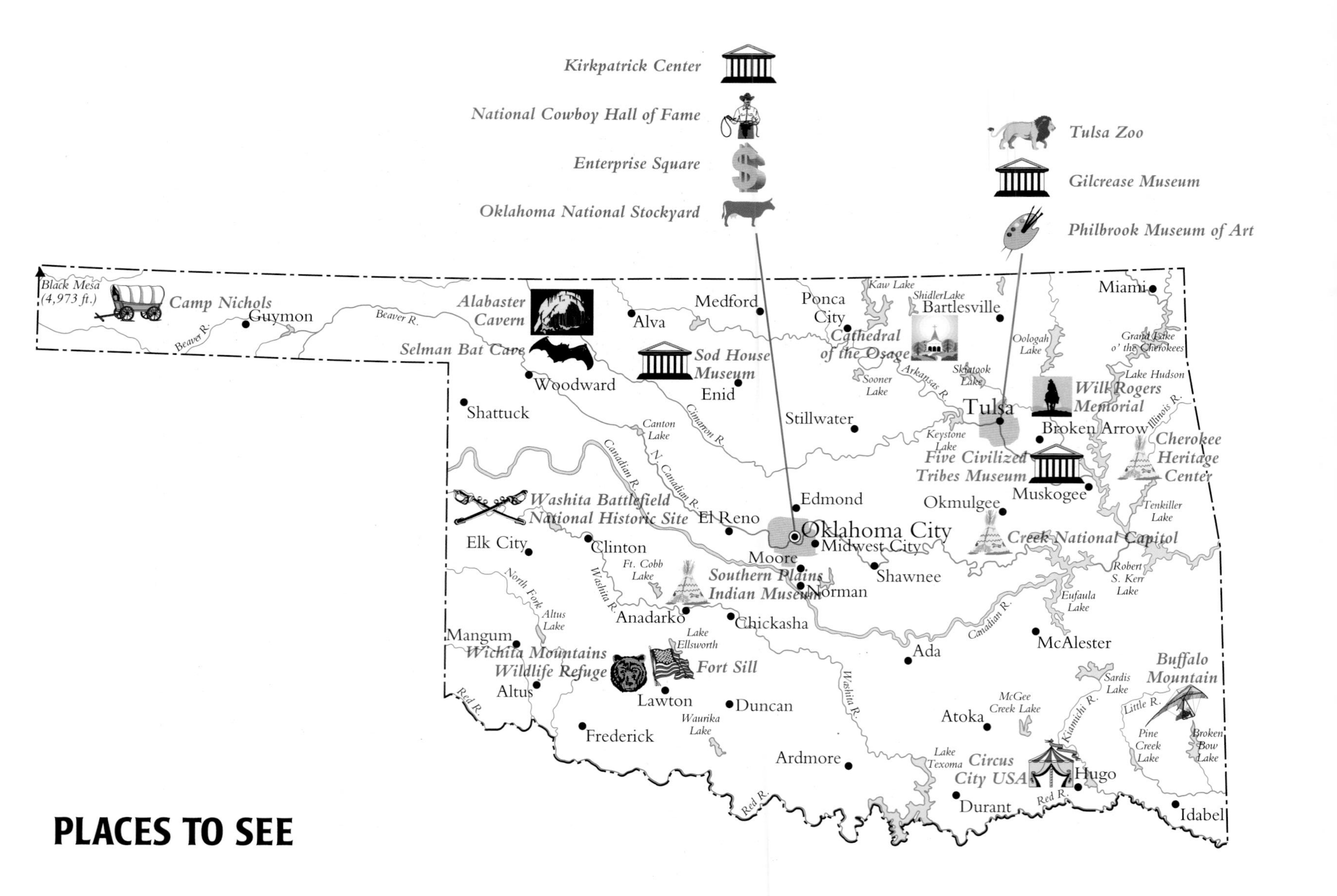

PLACES TO SEE

acres here, and have reconstructed the fantastic story of a civilization that flourished from about 800 to 1450. Not far from the mounds is Heavener Runestone State Park, where visitors may look over a large rock with eight "runes," or symbols, chiseled into its surface. The marks are undoubtedly old, but what they mean is argued about passionately. Some believe that Viking explorers carved the runestone during a journey from Scandinavia to the heart of North America almost a thousand years ago. Others say the Vikings never made the trip and think the symbols were carved by Frenchmen during the early 1700s—perhaps as a practical joke. The answer to the mystery will probably never be known, but Heavener is the place to go ponder it.

The Creek National Capitol is in Okmulgee. A sober building completed in 1878, it sits on the town square. In the 1920s, some Okmulgeeans thought the building looked old-fashioned and wanted to tear it down. "And what will you put in its place," asked Will Rogers—"a hotel, post office, hamburger stand, drug store?" Rogers helped save the capitol, a fact that today's Okmulgeeans appreciate. The fine old building now houses the Creek Indian Museum, well stocked with art and artifacts for visitors to discover. "If you can't find it anywhere else, it's here," proclaims museum director Debbie Martin. It's also the place where the tribal government holds its meetings.

And finally, Tulsa—the anchor of northeastern Oklahoma. Tulsa is "the most average city in the United States," writes sociologist Alan Wolfe. Companies use it to test their advertising campaigns. It's "a perfect place to find out whether Americans will use a new mouthwash or breakfast cereal." It's also America's third-biggest petroleum city. "Every major oil company has some root in Tulsa," says industry expert Wayne Swearington.

Because of oil, it's also beautiful. While western Oklahoma suffered during the Dust Bowl years, Tulsa oil millionaires built a forest of downtown buildings in the seductive Art Deco style. Zigzags, streamlined curves, and flamboyant decoration expressed

The cutting-edge architecture of the 1920s and 1930s was called Art Deco, and Tulsa, booming in those years, came away with one of the world's best collections of buildings in this ornate yet elegant style.

the builders' confidence that oil would make Tulsa a capital of modern elegance. "No one really realizes that outside of the area," says the "First Lady of Art Deco," Barbara Baer Capitman. "I have seen some of the best—absolutely best—examples of Deco buildings anywhere within a few blocks of downtown Tulsa. It's all over the city!"

LITTLE DIXIE

In Oklahoma's southeast corner, wild mountains, lakes, and farmland set off a scatter of interesting towns that remind people of the Deep South so much that the region is known as Little Dixie. Oklahomans love to camp, fish, and hike here, hoping for a glimpse of a bobcat or a flying squirrel. It's also a popular area for riding horses and mountain bikes. Buffalo Mountain has become a mecca for hang gliders. Just driving through this pretty territory on its twisting, scenic highways is a pleasure.

Below the foothills, in places like Beavers Pond Resort Park, the landscape turns swampy. Cypress trees dip their enormous roots into the Mountain Fork River, and visitors with visions of high, dry plains are amazed that this is part of Oklahoma, too.

Little Dixie is where you'll find Hugo, which calls itself Circus City, USA. "We're the largest tent circus in the world," boasts Jim Royal of the Carson and Barnes Circus, one of two old-fashioned traveling shows that spend winters in Hugo. Its rare Asian elephants still provide the muscle to raise the tents when the circus is on the road. Many circus performers settle down in Hugo when they retire. Their tombstones—often carved with elephants and other circus

Buffalo Mountain, near Talihina, is a top destination for hang gliders, who throw themselves off the mountain's spectacular cliffs.

images—dot the town's cemetery. "There's nothing left but empty popcorn sacks and wagon tracks," reads one. "The circus is gone."

THE SOUTHWESTERN PLAINS

The plains of southwest Oklahoma are notable not so much for one site or another but for the landscape in which they're all contained. It's mostly flat, mostly empty, mostly space. At a glance, it looks

GET YOUR KICKS

Route 66 is "the Mother Road" of American car travel. Snaking from Chicago to Los Angeles, the highway supported strips of motels, drive-ins, and bizarre roadside attractions back in the 1940s and 1950s when these were brand-new novelties. More than four hundred miles of the old road wind through Oklahoma—more than in any other state.

In many places, newer highways running alongside Route 66 now attract most of the traffic and business. Some of the bypassed towns, such as Clinton, celebrate the old car culture with events such as the Route 66 Festival. Others, such as Chandler, seem frozen in time. The cafes, gas stations, and motels are old, rusty, often closed up forever. Visiting them takes you back to days when cars had fins and whitewall tires, radios had to warm up before Elvis Presley or Chuck Berry could croon, and drivers all over the country believed that the place to "get their kicks" was Route 66.

like nothing could be concealed here—but a closer look reveals plenty of hidden treasures.

Visitors to this region will find Oklahoma's fourth-largest city, Lawton; a major army base, Fort Sill; and natural treasures such as the Wichita Mountains Wildlife Refuge. Bison, antelope, and elk share this big-skied preserve with prairie dogs and longhorn cattle. Farther west is the Washita Battlefield National Historic Site. The site, surrounded by the Black Kettle National Grassland, is where

TEN LARGEST CITIES

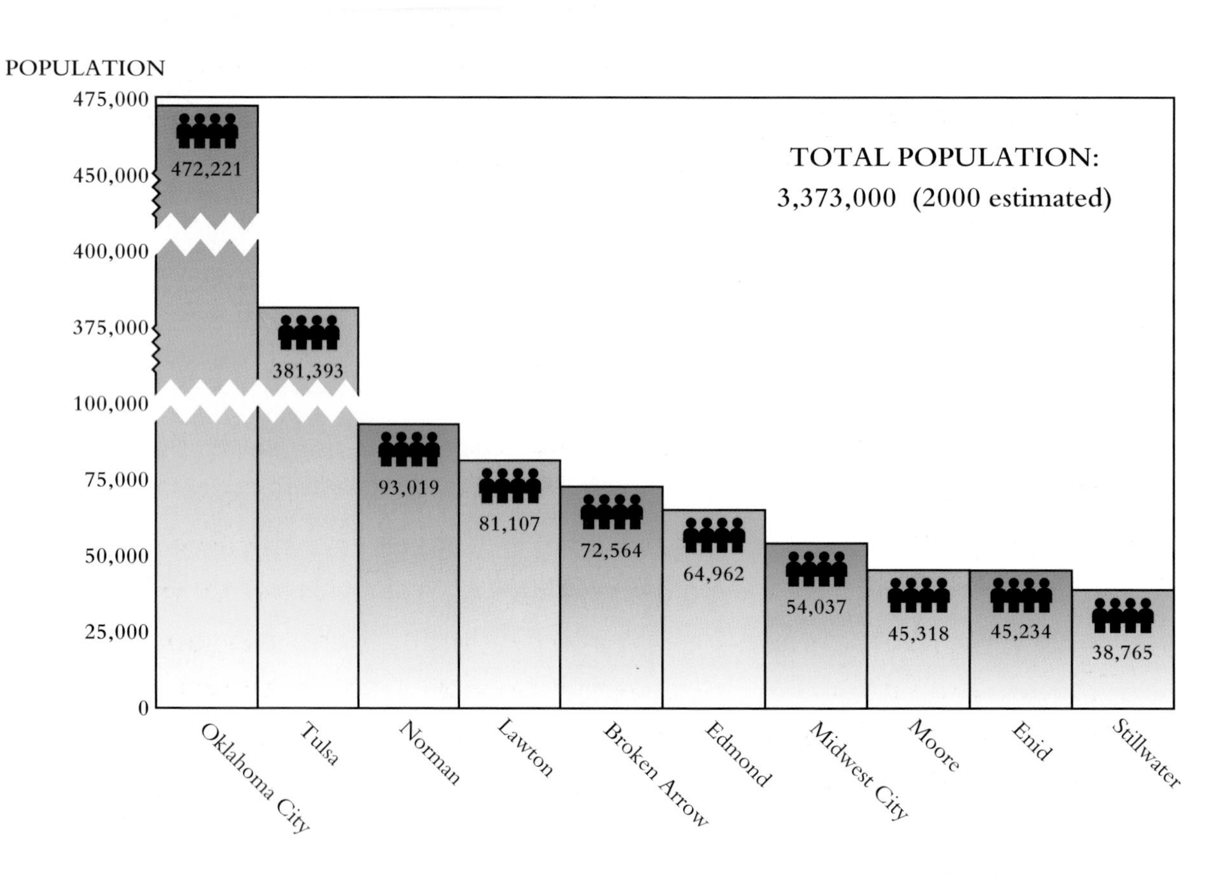

American general George Custer and eight hundred soldiers attacked a village in 1868, killing fifty or sixty Cheyenne Indians.

Anadarko is a central place on the southern plains. It's the headquarters of the Apache and Wichita tribes, and the home of the Southern Plains Indian Museum. Nearby is the National Hall of Fame for Famous American Indians, a solemn sculpture park of Indian heroes.

Anadarko's first settlers formed the Philomathic Society in order to share their experiences and escape the loneliness of frontier life. (*Philomathic* means "love of knowledge.") Thousands of objects—from Indian dolls to antique medical devices—were donated to the society over the years. These are displayed in a lively confusion of exhibits at Anadarko's Philomathic Pioneer Museum, which is housed in the old railroad station. Volunteers share the tales behind tools, costumes, photographs, and knickknacks, and will let a careful visitor examine them much more closely than in the average museum.

THE NORTHWEST AND THE PANHANDLE

The high, arid plains of Oklahoma's Panhandle and northwest are a "cultural boneyard," writes environmental historian Donald Worster, "where the evidences of bad judgment and misplaced schemes lie strewn about like bleached skulls." The very first decision about where to build a town could doom everyone involved to failure. "When people wanted to settle in a town," explains one Oklahoman, "they would go to the cemetery and look at the tombstones. If there weren't many recent dates or many

small children's graves they would know that the water was safe to drink and the town was a fairly good place to live." Even today, a visitor can look for such clues in the surviving towns of the western plains. A history of hard times, hard work, and fierce determination is carved into the streets and buildings and reflected in the faces of the people.

It's not hard to get the feel for those times in places like the Sod House Museum near Aline. Marshall McCully built the two-room structure in 1894 out of bricks of turf cut from the prairie. The interior is lined with sheets to keep the constant shower of dirt and bugs out of occupants' eyes. Most homesteaders abandoned their sod houses as soon as they could afford a "real" house, which makes the McCully place a rare sight. Sod houses could actually be quite comfortable—their thick walls kept them warm in the winter and cool in the fierce summer heat. The museum also features antique farm machinery and a blacksmith shop.

The Oklahoma Panhandle used to be called No Man's Land because it wasn't a part of any territory or state. This strip of dry, high land was finally assigned to Oklahoma, but the Panhandle still retains its own, distinctive style.

Near Boise City, at the very western tip of the Panhandle, is old Fort Nichols. It was a way station on the Santa Fe Trail—one of the most important early routes for western travel. Even today, visitors can spot the worn ruts carved by the wheels of passing wagons. Campsites

This windmill may look old-fashioned, but it's still practical technology on the arid, windy Panhandle, for thirsty cows—and dirty cowboys.

along Cold Spring Creek are marked by travelers' graffiti carved into the stone as far back as 1844. Some of these "autograph rocks" are covered with hundreds of names of long-departed travelers. Famed scout Kit Carson established a fort there in 1865 to protect travelers, but it was abandoned even before it was completed as the railroads

"Autograph cliffs" such as this one on the old Santa Fe Trail in Cimarron County were part graffiti wall and part bulletin board—travelers used them to assure friends and family who followed that they were safe.

ARNETT IN SUMMER

Oklahoma poet Patrick Worth Gray captures the scorched landscape of western Oklahoma in one of the many poems he has set in the northwest town of Arnett.

> Another Oklahoma town
> Hunkered down by a dry wash
> Cracked by drought in summer
> Heatwaves worming up from its convulsions.
> The black, sticky streets slither
> Like snakes, our car rattles,
> We shrink from the heat as though
> It is coiled. The dry air
> Crackles in our nostrils. We park
> And watch phantoms shimmer.

made trail travel obsolete. Fort Nichols completes the picture of a disappearing past, for little remains of it but the foundation.

SMACK DAB IN THE CENTER

Will Rogers once boasted that "Oklahoma is the heart, it's the vital organ of our national existence." At the heart of the heart is Oklahoma City, smack dab in the center of the state. Oklahoma's largest city was "born grown"—its population went from zero to thousands in a few hours during the first land rush on April 22, 1889. After more than a century, the capital still has some of the most fascinating features of any place in the state.

COW CHIP CAPITAL OF THE WORLD

One Panhandle town, Beaver, holds a festival every April that some people might avoid but others will find fascinating: the World Cow Chip Throwing Contest. In earlier days, pioneers in this nearly treeless area would gather cow manure for fuel, tossing the dried chips into their wagons as they worked. Today, people come from all over the country every April to sling the dung competitively. Most contestants claim to know the secret for success in this obscure sport. Ron Speer looks for chips from cows who eat buffalo grass; they stick together well, he says.

Nearly everyone enjoys the annual joke, but some, such as rancher Lloyd Barby, aren't inclined to compete. "I never throwed any," he explains, "because I walked in it all my life."

A majestic sculpted longhorn looks down over the entrance to the Oklahoma City Stockyards, home of the nation's busiest cattle auction. More than a hundred million cattle have passed through the stockyards on their way to a dinner plate.

Many of these are designed for kids. The Kirkpatrick Center is a collection of seven "kid-friendly" museums devoted to science, art, Indians, and photography. The National Cowboy Hall of Fame hosts the Chuck Wagon Gathering and Children's Cowboy Festival every May. Then there's Enterprise Square, a museum that celebrates American business. Visitors can learn about successful businesspeople and listen to singing dollar bills praise the virtues of economic competition.

Elsewhere in Oklahoma City you might want to visit Stockyards

City, the neighborhood that grew around the country's largest cattle auction operation. You can watch the animals parade into the auction ring and listen to the frenzied singsong of the auctioneers, then visit the western wear stores and antique shops around the corner.

Many newcomers are struck by the small-town friendliness of Oklahoma's largest city. "Clerks take time to say hello. It's not a 'keep your nose to the grindstone' attitude," says newcomer Jane Morilak. Friends and family don't necessarily understand her love affair with her adopted city. "Our daughter keeps sending us towels with cactuses on them," laughed Morilak. "She thinks we're living in the desert."

Misconceptions such as this often color outsiders' picture of Oklahoma. Most visitors see just a little and leave not quite understanding the place. Misleading images abound: land rushes, Dust Bowls, terrorist bombings. It takes more work to figure out what Oklahoma really is. Read more books. Or better yet, visit for yourself.

The Children's Cowboy Festival is just one of the many attractions at the National Cowboy Hall of Fame. Western art, music, and the annual Cowboy Poetry Gathering draw visitors to this unique feature of Oklahoma City.

THE FLAG: The Oklahoma flag shows an Osage warrior's shield against a blue background. Two symbols of peace—an olive branch and a peace pipe—cross the shield. The flag was adopted in 1925.

THE SEAL: The state seal, which was adopted in 1907, displays a white star. In its center, a frontiersman and an Indian shake hands, symbolizing cooperation among the people of Oklahoma. The star's five points contain the symbols of the Cherokee, Choctaw, Chickasaw, Seminole and Creek Nations, five tribes that settled in Oklahoma. Around the star are arrayed 45 stars, representing the states in the Union when Oklahoma became the 46th state.

STATE SURVEY

Statehood: November 16, 1907

Origin of Name: From the Choctaw words *okla*, meaning "people," and *homma*, meaning "red"

Scissor-tailed flycatcher

Nickname: Sooner State

Capital: Oklahoma City

Motto: Labor Conquers All Things

Bird: Scissor-tailed flycatcher

Flower: Mistletoe

Tree: Redbud

Animal: American buffalo

Fish: White or sand bass

Grass: Indian grass

Mistletoe

OKLAHOMA

The 1942 Broadway musical *Oklahoma!* has remained one of the most popular shows ever produced. it was based on the play *Green Grow the Lilacs* by Lynn Riggs and tells the story of the conflicts between the cowboy and the farmer in late-nineteenth-century Oklahoma Territory. This song was one of the many hits from the show. It was adopted by the Oklahoma legislature as the official state song in 1953.

Reptile: Mountain boomer lizard

Rock: Barite rose rock

Wildflower: Indian blanket

Country-and-Western Song: "Faded Love," by Bob Wills and John Willis

GEOGRAPHY

Highest Point: 4,973 feet above sea level, at Black Mesa

Lowest Point: 287 feet above sea level, along the Little River in McCurtain County

Area: 69,903 square miles

Greatest Distance, North to South: 231 miles

Greatest Distance, East to West: 478 miles

Bordering States: Colorado and Kansas to the north, Missouri and Arkansas to the east, Texas to the south, New Mexico to the west

Hottest Recorded Temperature: 120°F at Alva on July 18, 1936; at Altus on July 19, 1936, and August 12, 1936; at Poteau on August 10, 1936; and at Tishomingo on July 26, 1943

Coldest Recorded Temperature: -27°F at Vinita on February 13, 1905, and at Watts on January 18, 1930

Average Annual Precipitation: 33 inches

Major Rivers: Arkansas, Beaver, Blue, Canadian, Chikaskia, Cimarron, Kiamichi, Little, Mountain Fork, Neosho, Poteau, Red, Salt Fork, Verdigris, Washita

Major Lakes: Atoka, Broken Bow, Eufala, Fort Gibson, Foss, Great Salt Plains, Kaw, Lake o' the Cherokees, Oologah, Pine Creek, Sardis, Tenkiller, Texoma, Thunderbird, Waurika

Trees: ash, cedar, cottonwood, elm, hickory, maple, pecan, pine, sweet gum, walnut

Wild Plants: bluestem, buffalo grass, dogwood, goldenrod, Indian grass, mesquite, petunia, primrose, sagebrush, sunflower, verbena, violet, wild indigo

Animals: armadillo, bat, coyote, deer, elk, gray fox, mink, opossum, otter, prairie dog, rabbit, raccoon, red fox, squirrel

Coyote

Birds: blue jay, cardinal, crow, dove, duck, meadowlark, mockingbird, oriole, owl, roadrunner, robin, sparrow, thrush

Fish: bass, buffalo fish, carp, catfish, crappie, drumfish, paddlefish, sunfish

Endangered Animals: American burying beetle, black-capped vireo, Eskimo curlew, gray bat, Indiana bat, least tern, Ouachita rock pocketbook, Ozark big-eared bat, red-cockaded woodpecker, whooping crane

Red-cockaded woodpecker

TIMELINE

Oklahoma History

c. A.D. 1200 The Spiro people build huge mounds in what is now eastern Oklahoma

1500s Many Indian tribes, including the Arapaho, Caddo, Kiowa, Osage, Pawnee, and Wichita, live in present-day Oklahoma

1541 A party led by Spaniard Francisco Vásquez de Coronado crosses

Oklahoma while searching for gold, becoming the first Europeans to set foot in the region

1682 France claims Oklahoma

1714 Juchereau de St. Denis becomes the first Frenchman to set foot in Oklahoma

1762 France cedes Louisiana, which includes Oklahoma, to Spain

1800 Spain cedes Louisiana back to France

1803 Most of Oklahoma becomes U.S. territory as part of the Louisiana Purchase

1824 Forts Gibson and Townsend, the region's first military posts, are built

1825 Much of Oklahoma is designated Indian Territory and is set aside for Indians

1830–1842 Thousands of Cherokee, Choctaw, Chickasaw, Creek, and Seminole Indians are forced into Oklahoma from their homes in the Southeast

1844 The *Cherokee Advocate*, Oklahoma's first newspaper, begins publishing in Tahlequah

1861–1865 Many people in Indian Territory support the Confederacy during the Civil War

1867 Texas cowboys make the first great cattle drive up the Chisholm Trail across Oklahoma to stockyards in Kansas

1872 The Missouri-Kansas-Texas Railroad, the first railroad across present-day Oklahoma, is completed

1889 Parts of Oklahoma are opened to white settlement; on April 22, 50,000 people move to Oklahoma in its first land rush

1890 The Territory of Oklahoma is established; Oklahoma State University is founded

1897 Oklahoma's first significant oil well is drilled near Bartlesville

1907 Oklahoma becomes the 46th state; the state prohibits the sale of alcohol

1910 Oklahoma City becomes the state capital

1921 As many as 300 African Americans are killed in Tulsa in one of the nation's worst incidents of racial violence

1928 The vast Oklahoma City oil field is opened

1930s In what is known as the Dust Bowl, severe drought and high winds cause massive dust storms, forcing hundreds of thousands of people to leave the state

1941–1945 The United States participates in World War II

1959 The state's prohibition of alcohol is repealed

1970 The Arkansas River Navigation System is completed, allowing barges to travel all the way to Tulsa from the Gulf of Mexico

1982 Oklahoma suffers as oil prices decline drastically

1990 Oklahoma becomes the first state to limit the number of terms its state legislators may serve

1995 A terrorist bomb blows up a federal office building in Oklahoma City, killing 168 people

Pecan harvest

ECONOMY

Agricultural Products: beef cattle, catfish, chickens, corn, cotton, eggs, hay, hogs, milk, peaches, peanuts, pecans, sorghum, soybeans, turkeys, wheat

Manufactured Products: aircraft equipment, electronic components, food products, machinery, metal products, television parts, tires

Natural Resources: coal, crushed stone, iodine, natural gas, oil, sand and gravel

Business and Trade: banking, insurance, real estate, wholesale and retail trade

CALENDAR OF CELEBRATIONS

International Finals Rodeo Before watching the dust fly as some of the world's best cowboys compete in bull riding, steer wrestling, and other competitions,

International Finals Rodeo

check out the huge parade of horses, wagons, and musicians that opens this January rodeo in Oklahoma City.

Bitter Creek Frontier Daze People dressed as outlaws, sheriffs, cowboys, and soldiers depict life in 19th-century Oklahoma during this festival near Watonga each February.

Weatherford World Championship Hog Calling Contest Each spring, hog callers from around the world travel to the small town of Weatherford to show off their best oinks and soo-wees. Afterwards, they can eat their fill of barbecue.

Azalea Festival At this April festival in Muskogee, visitors can admire 40 acres of brightly blooming azaleas.

Red Earth Cultural Festival This June event in Oklahoma City calls itself the World's Biggest Powwow. Members of more than a hundred different tribes participate in the dancing competitions and exhibitions. Visitors also enjoy parades, art shows, and lots of delicious food.

Pecan Festival Five million pounds of pecans are harvested in Okmulgee County each year. In June the town of Okmulgee honors its favorite nut with a festival that has produced the world's largest pecan pie, largest pecan cookie, and largest pecan brownie.

Kiamichi Owa Chito Festival of the Forest Outdoor events such as canoe racing and chainsaw carving are the big draws at this June extravaganza in Beavers Bend Resort Park.

Ada Air Expo At this July festival in Ada, people take to the sky any way they can. Some are in hot air balloons, others are in airplanes, and still others are wafting to the ground with parachutes.

Cherokee National Holiday Besides a powwow, arts and crafts displays, and workshops, this September event in Tahlequah includes the state of the nation speech by the principal chief of the Cherokee Nation.

Watonga Cheese Festival Each October Watonga is the site of cheese tastings, historical reenactments, and an art show.

Chickasha Festival of Light During the Christmas season millions of lights give Chickasha a festive feeling.

STATE STARS

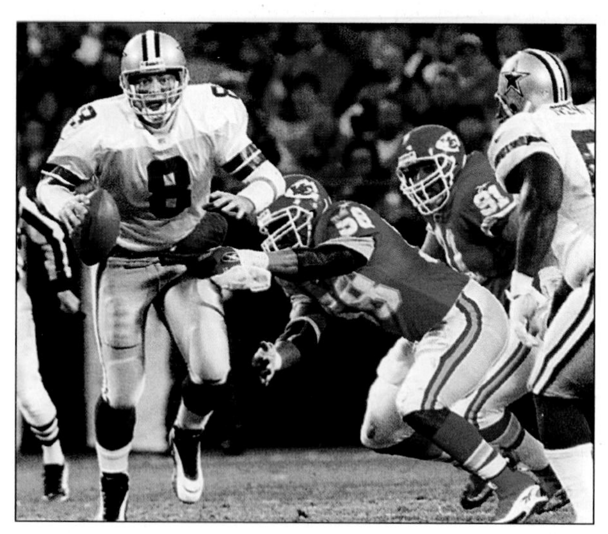

Troy Aikman

Troy Aikman (1966–   ) is one of the leading quarterbacks in the National Football League. An extraordinary passer, he led the Dallas Cowboys to three Super Bowl victories in four years. Aikman was born in California and spent much of his youth in Henryetta, Oklahoma.

Johnny Bench (1947–   ), one of baseball's best catchers, was born in Oklahoma City. He earned the National League Rookie of the Year Award in 1968. An excellent defensive player, Bench won 10 consecutive Gold Glove awards. He was also a big offensive threat, leading the league in home runs twice and in runs batted in three times. Bench helped the

Cincinnati Reds win the World Series in 1975 and 1976. He was elected to the National Baseball Hall of Fame in 1989.

Johnny Bench

Garth Brooks

Garth Brooks (1962–) is one of the world's most popular country singers. His 1991 album *Ropin' the Wind* was the first country album to reach number one on the pop charts the week it came out. Brooks, who is famous for his energetic live shows, is one of the best-selling acts in music history. He has had more than 20 number-one hits, including "Friends in Low Places" and "Rodeo." Brooks was born in Tulsa.

Charlie Christian (1916–1942) was an influential jazz electric guitarist. Christian played sophisticated music on his electric guitar, performing solos that were more like what horn players usually played. His style and improvisations influenced jazz guitarists for decades. Christian grew up in Oklahoma City.

Ralph Ellison

Ralph Ellison (1914–1994), a native of Oklahoma City, wrote *Invisible Man*, which is generally considered one of the greatest American novels of the 20th century. The novel describes a young black man's travels as he searches for his identity and for acceptance. The man comes to realize that as an African American, he is ignored—he's invisible to society. Both brutal and honest, realistic and dreamlike, *Invisible Man* earned Ellison the National Book Award in 1953. Ellison, who also published essays and short stories to great acclaim, was awarded the Medal of Freedom, the nation's highest civilian honor, in 1969.

Woody Guthrie (1912–1967), a native of Okemah, was an influential folk singer. As a 16-year-old, Guthrie left home to play guitar with a traveling magic show. He ended up in California, where he often performed at migrant labor camps. Guthrie eventually published more than a thousand songs, often about people facing hard times. His most famous is probably "This Land Is Your Land." Guthrie's autobiography, *Bound for Glory*, is a classic tale of life during the depression.

Tony Hillerman (1925–   ), one of the nation's most successful mystery writers, was born in Sacred Heart and attended the University of Oklahoma. Later, he moved to New Mexico, where he became fascinated by Navajo Indian culture. His novels, such as *Skinwalkers* and *The Thief of Time*, are both exciting mysteries and careful examinations of Navajo traditions and contemporary life.

Allan Houser (1914–1994) was a leading sculptor who pushed Native American sculpture in modern directions. A Chiracahua Apache, Houser depicted traditional Indians such as warriors in a variety of materials, including bronze, steel, stone, and alabaster. In 1992, he became the first Indian to receive the National Medal of the Arts, the nation's highest award for artistic achievement. Houser was born in Apache.

Karl Jansky (1905–1950), who was born in Norman, founded radio astronomy—the study of distant objects by the radio waves they emit. An electrical engineer, Jansky was trying to reduce the static that often interrupted long-distance radio transmissions. In 1932, he discovered that the steady hiss was the result of radio waves that seemed to come from the center of the galaxy. Previously, it was thought that all radio waves were produced by people. In recognition of his contribution, today the unit used to measure the intensity of radio waves is called the jansky.

William Wayne Keeler (1908–1987) was both a chief of the Cherokee Nation and the chief executive officer of Phillips Petroleum. Keeler spent his entire career with Phillips Petroleum, working his way up to become president and chief executive officer in 1967, positions he held until he retired in 1987. After he became the Cherokee chief in 1949, he founded the first Cherokee National Holiday and organized the Cherokee National Historical Society. He also helped the Cherokee win back land that had been taken from them by the U.S. government. Keeler grew up in Bartlesville.

Shannon Lucid (1943–), an astronaut who grew up in Bethany, holds the American record for the longest stay in space. Lucid attended the University of Oklahoma and became a biochemist. She had already been on four space missions when the space shuttle *Atlantis* brought her to the

Russian *Mir* space station in 1996. Lucid stayed on *Mir* for 188 days, 4 hours—longer than any other American has spent in space.

Wilma Mankiller (1945–), who was born in Stilwell, was the first female principal chief of the Cherokee Nation. After becoming chief in 1985, Mankiller worked to improve health care and education and fostered many community self-help programs. Under her leadership, the number of members in the tribe tripled.

Mickey Mantle

Mickey Mantle (1931–1995), a native of Spavinaw, was one of baseball's greatest hitters. He played centerfield for the New York Yankees for 18 years, helping them win 7 World Series. A great switch hitter, Mantle ranks eighth in career home runs with 536. This three-time American League Most Valuable Player had his best year in 1956, when he led the league in home runs, runs batted in, and batting average. Mantle was elected to the National Baseball Hall of Fame in 1974.

Reba McEntire (1955–) is one of the nation's most popular country singers. With her great range and a voice that can be both velvety and sassy, she has hit number one on the charts many times with songs such as "How Blue" and "Somebody Should Leave." McEntire was born in Chockie.

N. Scott Momaday (1934–), a member of the Kiowa tribe, became the first Native American to win the

Reba McEntire

Pulitzer Prize for fiction when his book *House Made of Dawn* was awarded the honor in 1969. The novel is the story of a World War II veteran who is struggling to find his place in both the Indian and non-Indian worlds. Some of Momaday's other works, such as *The Way to Rainy Mountain*, have retold Kiowa legends. Momaday was born in Lawton.

Frank Phillips (1873–1950) moved to Bartlesville in 1903 from his home in Iowa to drill for oil. In 1917, he founded Phillips Petroleum Company, which grew into one of the nation's largest oil companies.

Will Rogers (1879–1935) was one of the most popular entertainers of the early 20th century. Born in Oologah, he began his career as a trick roper in Wild West shows before moving on to vaudeville. He eventually became a tremendously popular radio personality and newspaper columnist, famous for his gentle, folksy humor. Rogers also appeared in more than 70 films, including *State Fair*, *Life Begins at Forty*, and *Judge Priest*.

Maria Tallchief (1925–) was one of first American ballerinas to gain international acclaim. Famed for her technical precision, subtlety, and emotion, she was the prima ballerina of the New York City Ballet from 1947 to 1960. She is perhaps best remembered for her performance as the Sugar Plum Fairy in *The Nutcracker*. After her retirement in 1965, Tallchief turned her attention to teaching. In 1979, she founded the Chicago City Ballet. Tallchief, who is half Osage, was born in Fairfax.

Maria Tallchief

Jim Thorpe

Jim Thorpe (1887–1953), a Sac and Fox Indian from Prague, is considered the greatest athlete of the first half of the 20th century. At the 1912 Olympics, he dominated the track and field competition, winning the gold medal in both the pentathlon and the decathlon. But the following year, he was stripped of his medals because he had played semiprofessional baseball when he was younger. At the time, the Olympics only allowed amateur athletes. Thorpe later became a professional baseball and football player. In 1920, he became the president of the American Professional Football Association, which would become the National Football League. Many years after Thorpe's death, the International Olympic Committee gave duplicate gold medals to his children, realizing they should never have been taken away.

Alfre Woodard (1953–) is an acclaimed actress, renowned for her consistently strong, controlled performances. Woodard has a remarkable range, playing funny, wise, wary, and every other state with equal skill. She has appeared in such films as *Passion Fish*, *Crooklyn*, and *Bopha!* She has also won Emmy Awards for her performances in the television series *Hill Street Blues* and *L.A. Law*. Woodard was born in Tulsa.

Alfre Woodard

TOUR THE STATE

Cherokee Heritage Center (Tahlequah) At this site you can tour a replica of a 17th-century Cherokee village and see a play about the disastrous Trail of Tears. You can also watch demonstrations of soap making, weaving, and other traditional skills.

Will Rogers Memorial (Claremore) A large statue of the famous entertainer graces the town that Rogers called home.

Will Rogers Memorial

Tenkiller State Park (Vian) Hiking, fishing, camping, scuba diving—this park is the perfect place to enjoy the outdoors.

Talimena Scenic Byway (Talihina) Sharp curves and stunning vistas dot this tour of the Ouachita National Forest. In the spring wildflowers and dogwood blooms color the roadside, while in the fall the brilliant golds and rusts of the changing leaves take over.

Gilcrease Museum (Tulsa) One of the nation's best collections of western art, this museum contains everything from Indian art made more than a thousand years ago to works by such renowned western artists as George Catlin.

Tulsa Zoo (Tulsa) A highlight of this zoo is the rain forest exhibit, where colorful birds flit around your head while lizards and other creatures move among the lush plants.

Philbrook Museum of Art (Tulsa) After checking out the wide-ranging art housed in this beautiful mansion, many visitors enjoy strolling through its gardens past sparkling ponds.

Mac's Antique Car Museum (Tulsa) Fifty-one carefully restored cars are on exhibit at this museum, including a 1912 Model T.

Tallgrass Prairie Preserve (Pawhuska) Buffalo roam this preserve, where some grasses grow eight feet high. You might also spy bobcats and beavers, antelope and armadillos.

Cathedral of the Osage (Pawhuska) Many of the exquisite stained glass windows of this church depict Native Americans.

State Museum of History (Oklahoma City) At this museum, visitors can see all sorts of artifacts of Oklahoma's history, including a real buffalo-hide tepee, a wagon that was used in the land rush, and many oil-drilling tools.

Omniplex (Oklahoma City) You can climb inside a molecule, tour a human body, figure out what causes lightning, or try out hundreds of other interactive exhibits at this fascinating museum.

Oklahoma National Stockyards (Oklahoma City) Listen to the rapid-fire auctions and watch the cowboys on horseback manage the cattle at the center of the Oklahoma cattle industry.

National Cowboy Hall of Fame (Oklahoma City) All aspects of the West, not just cowboys, are honored at this museum. You'll see exhibits on Native Americans, rodeos, and movie Westerns. You can even explore a replica of a frontier town.

Southern Plains Indian Museum (Anadarko) Outstanding traditional arts and contemporary crafts are on display at this museum.

Wichita Mountains Wildlife Refuge (Holy City) Elk, bison, bobcats, and even longhorn cattle make their home in the nation's oldest managed wildlife preserve.

Fort Sill (Lawton) This fort, founded in 1869, abounds with history. You can see the guardhouse where the great Apache warrior Geronimo was held prisoner, as well as displays on Quanah Parker, the last Comanche leader to remain free. Also on the grounds is the cemetery where Geronimo, Parker, and many other famous Indians are buried.

Alabaster Caverns State Park (Freedom) Visitors who hike deep into the colorful caverns will see all sorts of crystals and minerals, but the highlight is the beautiful black alabaster, which is found in only two other caves in the world.

Little Sahara State Park (Waynoka) The roar of dune buggies and motorcycles greet visitors at this park, where hundreds of acres of sand dunes shift as the strong wind blows.

Selman Bat Cave (Freedom) Most evenings in July and August, you can watch a million Mexican free-tailed bats head out from this cave for a night of feasting on insects. They eat about 10 tons of insects every night.

Black Mesa State Park and Nature Preserve (Kenton) A hike to Oklahoma's highest point offers an extraordinary view of the Panhandle and beyond. Before you head up, make sure you stop to look at the dinosaur tracks.

FUN FACTS

Oklahoma is called the Sooner State because some of the settlers in the first land rush in 1889 jumped the gun. They snuck out early to stake their claims, getting to the prime land "sooner" than they should have.

The world's first parking meter was installed in Oklahoma City on July 16, 1935.

Oklahoma City was also the site of the first shopping cart. Grocery store owner Sylvan Goldman noticed that customers were having trouble carrying baskets and watching their children, so he came up with the idea of basket carriers on wheels. No one used them until he hired people to push them around the store so other folks would see how useful they were.

FIND OUT MORE

Books, newspapers, films, and websites can all take you farther into Oklahoma. Here are some suggestions for starting that journey.

GENERAL STATE BOOKS

Fradin, Dennis Brindell. *Oklahoma.* Danbury, CT: Children's Press, 1995.

Ladoux, Rita C. *Oklahoma.* Minneapolis, MN: Lerner, 1997.

Reedy, Jerry, Jean F. Blashfield, and Ann Heinrichs. *Oklahoma.* Danbury, CT: Children's Press, 1998.

Thompson, Kathleen. *Oklahoma.* Austin, TX: Raintree Steck-Vaughan, 1996.

SPECIAL INTEREST BOOKS

Antle, Nancy. *Beautiful Land: A Story of the Oklahoma Land Rush.* New York: Viking, 1994.

Lamb, Nancy. *One April Morning: Children Remember the Oklahoma City Bombing.* New York: Lothrop, Lee and Shepard, 1996.

FICTION

Ferber, Edna. *Cimarron.* New York: Doubleday, 1930. This is a classic Western about settlers on the western Oklahoma plains.

Grove, Vicki. *The Starplace.* New York: Putnam's Sons, 1999. Eighth-graders confront segregation in Quiver, Oklahoma, in 1961.

Hesse, Karen. *Out of the Dust.* New York: Scholastic, 1999. Award-winning novel in verse about the courage of a girl confronting tragedy in Dust Bowl Oklahoma.

Rawls, Wilson. *Summer of the Monkeys.* New York: Dell, 1999. A boy discovers monkeys—yes, monkeys—on his family's Oklahoma homestead.

FILMS

The Grapes of Wrath. Twentieth Century Fox, 1940. This classic about Dust Bowl Okies is one of the twenty-five best American movies of all time, according to the American Film Institute.

Oklahoma! Twentieth Century Fox, 1956. Another classic, in the musical genre. Check it out for its historical mistakes and its great songs.

Echoes across the Prairie: The Vanishing Black West. WRS, Inc., 1998. This movie documents the history of the all-black towns founded in Oklahoma, 13 of which still exist today.

First Person Singular: John Hope Franklin. PBS Home Video, 1997. A documentary dwelling on Franklin's life in Oklahoma as well as his career as a leading scholar of African America.

MUSIC

Woody Guthrie: Library of Congress Recordings. UNI-Rounder, 1988. In these unique recordings from 1940, Guthrie recounts his childhood in Okemah and the terrible story of the Dust Bowl in song and words.

WEBSITES

http://www.oklahoman.com is the website of the *Daily Oklahoman*, Oklahoma's leading newspaper. Besides offering the day's news, this site has great links to other Oklahoma websites, including some designed by and for children.

http://www.oklaosf.state.ok.us is the state's official website. Go there to learn about the government and the economy, and to find links to lots more Oklahoma websites.

INDEX

Page numbers for illustrations are in boldface.